The Articulate Executive

THE ARTICULATE EXECUTIVE

Improving Written, Interpersonal, and Group Communication

A Harvard Business Review Paperback

Harvard Business Review paperback No. 90036

The *Harvard Business Review* articles in this collection
are available as individual reprints, with the exception of
"Management Communication and the Grapevine." Discounts
apply to quantity purchases. For information and ordering
contact Operations Department, Harvard Business School
Publishing Division, Boston, MA 02163. Telephone: (617)
495-6192, 9 a.m. to 5 p.m. EST. Fax: (617) 495-6985 24 hours
a day.

Editor's Note: Some articles in this book may have been
written before authors and editors began to take into consideration the role of women in management. We hope the
archaic usage representing all managers as male does not
detract from the usefulness of the collection.

Contents

Effective Communication in Groups

Effective Job Interviewing

Effective
Business Writing

Managers the nation over
ask, or have to answer —

"What do you mean
I can't write?"

By John Fielden

What do businessmen answer when they are asked, "What's the most troublesome problem you have to live with?" Frequently they reply, "People just can't write! What do they learn in college now? When I was a boy . . . !"

There is no need to belabor this point; readers know well how true it is. HBR subscribers, for example, recently rated the "ability to communicate" as the prime requisite of a promotable executive (see EXHIBIT I).[1] And, of all the aspects of communication, the written form is the most troublesome, if only because of its formal nature. It is received cold, without the communicator's tone of voice or gesture to help. It is rigid; it cannot be adjusted to the recipients' reactions as it is being delivered. It stays "on the record," and cannot be undone. Further, the reason it is in fact committed to paper is usually that its subject is considered too crucial or significant to be entrusted to casual, short-lived verbal form.

Businessmen know that the ability to write well is a highly valued asset in a top executive. Consequently, they become ever more conscious of their writing ability as they consider what qualities they need in order to rise in their company.

They know that in big business today ideas are not exchanged exclusively by word of mouth (as they might be in smaller businesses). And they know that even if they get oral approval for something they wish to do, there will be the inevitable "give me a memo on it" concluding

[1] See also, C. Wilson Randle, "How to Identify Promotable Executives," HBR May–June 1956, p. 122.

remark that will send them back to their office to oversee the writing of a carefully documented report.

They know, too, that as they rise in their company, they will have to be able to supervise the writing of subordinates — for so many of the memos, reports, and letters written by subordinates will go out over their signature, or be passed on to others in the company and thus reflect on the caliber of work done under their supervision.

Even the new data-processing machines will not make business any less dependent on words. For while the new machines are fine for handling tabular or computative work, someone must write up an eventual analysis of the findings in the common parlance of the everyday executive.

Time for Action

Complaints about the inability of managers to write are a very common and justifiable refrain. But the problem this article poses — and seeks to solve — is that it is of very little use to complain about something and stop right there. I think it is about time for managers to begin to do something about it. And the first step is *to define what "it" — what good business writing — really is.*

Suppose you are a young managerial aspirant who has recently been told: "You simply can't write!" What would this mean to you? Naturally, you would be hurt, disappointed, perhaps even alarmed to have your *own* nagging doubts about your writing ability put uncomfortably on the line. "Of course," you say, "I know I'm no stylist. I don't even pretend to be a literarily inclined person. But how can I improve my writing on the job? Where do I begin? Exactly what *is* wrong with my writing?" But nobody tells you in specific, meaningful terms.

Does this mean that you can't spell or punctuate or that your grammar is disastrous? Does it mean that you can't think or organize your thoughts? Or does it mean that even though you are scrupulously correct in grammar and tightly organized in your thinking, a report or letter from you is always completely unreadable; that reading it, in effect, is like trying to butt one's head through a brick wall? Or does it mean that you are so tactless and boorish in the human relations aspect of communication that your messages actually build resentment and resistance? Do you talk "down" too much or do you talk "over your reader's head"? Just what do you do wrong?

Merely being told that you can't write is so basically meaningless and so damaging to your morale that you may end up writing more ineffectually than ever before. What you need to know is: "What are the elements of good business writing? And in which of these elements am I proficient? In which do I fall down?" If only the boss could break his complaint down into a more meaningful set of components, you could begin to do something about them.

Now let's shift and assume that you are a high-ranking manager whose job it is to supervise a staff of assistants. What can you do about upgrading the writing efforts of your men? You think of the time lost by having to do reports and letters over and over before they go out, the feasibility reports which did not look so feasible after having been befogged by an ineffectual writer, the letters presented for your signature that would have infuriated the receiver had you let them be mailed. But where are you to start?

Here is where the interests of superior and subordinate meet. Unless both arrive at a common understanding, a shared vocabulary that enables them to communicate with one another about the writing jobs that need to be done, nobody is going to get very far. No oversimplified, gimmicky slogans (such as, "Every letter is a sales letter"; "Accentuate the positive, eliminate the negative"; or "Write as you speak") are going to serve this purpose. No partial view is either — whether that of the English teacher, the logician, or the social scientist — since good business writing is not just grammar, or clear thinking, or winning friends

EXHIBIT I. QUALITIES THAT CHARACTERIZE PROMOTABLE EXECUTIVES

SOURCE: Taken from EXHIBIT III, Garda W. Bowman, "What Helps or Harms Promotability?" (Problems in Review), HBR January–February 1964, p. 14.

and influencing people. It is some of each, the proportion depending on the purpose.

Total Inventory

To know what effective business writing is, we need a total inventory of all its aspects, so that:

• Top managers can say to their training people, "Are you sure our training efforts in written communications are not tackling just part of the problem? Are we covering all aspects of business writing?"

• A superior can say to an assistant, "Here, look; this is where you are weak. See? It is one thing when you write letters that you sign, another when you write letters that I sign. The position and power of the person we are writing to make a lot of difference in *what* we say and *how* we say it."

• The young manager can use the inventory as a guide to self-improvement (perhaps even ask his superior to go over his writing with him, using the writing inventory as a means of assuring a common critical vocabulary).

• The superior may himself get a few hints about how he might improve his own performance.

Such an inventory appears in EXHIBIT II. Notice that it contains four basic categories — *readability, correctness, appropriateness,* and *thought.* Considerable effort has gone into making these categories (and the subtopics under them) as mutually exclusive as possible, although some overlap is inevitable. But even if they are not completely exclusive, they are still far less general than an angry, critical remark, such as, "You cannot write."

Furthermore, you should understand that these four categories are not listed in order of importance, since their importance varies according to the abilities and the duties of each individual. The same thing is true of the subtopics; I shall make no attempt to treat each of them equally, but will simply try to do some practical, commonsense highlighting. I will begin with readability, and discuss it most fully, because this is an area where half-truths abound and need to be scotched before introducing the other topics.

Readability

What is *readability?* Nothing more than a clear style of writing. It does not result absolutely (as some readability experts would have you believe) from mathematical counts of syllables, of sentence length, or of abstract words. These inflexible approaches to readability assume that all writing is being addressed to a general audience. Consequently, their greatest use is in forming judgments about the readability of such things as mass magazine editorial copy, newspaper communications, and elementary textbooks.

To prove this point, all you need do is to pick up a beautifully edited magazine like the *New England Journal of Medicine* and try to read an article in it. You as a layman will probably have trouble. On the other hand, your physician will tell you that the article is a masterpiece of readable exposition. But, on second look, you will still find it completely unreadable. The reason, obviously, is that you do not have the background or the vocabulary necessary to understand it. The same thing would hold true if you were to take an article from a management science quarterly, say, one dealing with return on investment or statistical decision making, and give it to the physician. Now he is likely to judge this one to be completely incomprehensible, while you may find it the most valuable and clear discussion of the topic you have ever seen.

In situations like this, it does not make much difference whether the sentences are long or short; if the reader does not have the background to understand the material, he just doesn't. And writing such specialized articles according to the mathematical readability formulas is not going to make them clearer.

Nevertheless, it is true that unnecessarily long, rambling sentences are wearing to read. Hence you will find these stylistic shortcomings mentioned in EXHIBIT II. The trick a writer has to learn is to judge the complexity and the abstractness of the material he is dealing with, and to cut his sentences down in those areas where the going is especially difficult. It also helps to stick to a direct subject-verb-object construction in sentences wherever it is important to communicate precisely. Flights of unusually dashing style should be reserved for those sections which are quite general in nature and concrete in subject matter.

What about paragraphs? The importance of "paragraph construction" is often overlooked in business communication, but few things are more certain to make the heart sink than the sight of page after page of unbroken type. One

EXHIBIT II. WRITTEN PERFORMANCE INVENTORY

1. READABILITY

READER'S LEVEL

- [ ] Too specialized in approach
- [ ] Assumes too great a knowledge of subject
- [ ] So underestimates the reader that it belabors the obvious

SENTENCE CONSTRUCTION

- [ ] Unnecessarily long in difficult material
- [ ] Subject-verb-object word order too rarely used
- [ ] Choppy, overly simple style (in simple material)

PARAGRAPH CONSTRUCTION

- [ ] Lack of topic sentences
- [ ] Too many ideas in single paragraph
- [ ] Too long

FAMILIARITY OF WORDS

- [ ] Inappropriate jargon
- [ ] Pretentious language
- [ ] Unnecessarily abstract

READER DIRECTION

- [ ] Lack of "framing" (i.e., failure to tell the reader about purpose and direction of forthcoming discussion)
- [ ] Inadequate transitions between paragraphs
- [ ] Absence of subconclusions to summarize reader's progress at end of divisions in the discussion

FOCUS

- [ ] Unclear as to subject of communication
- [ ] Unclear as to purpose of message

2. CORRECTNESS

MECHANICS

- [ ] Shaky grammar
- [ ] Faulty punctuation

FORMAT

- [ ] Careless appearance of documents
- [ ] Failure to use accepted company form

COHERENCE

- [ ] Sentences seem awkward owing to illogical and ungrammatical yoking of unrelated ideas
- [ ] Failure to develop a logical progression of ideas through coherent, logically juxtaposed paragraphs

3. APPROPRIATENESS

A. UPWARD COMMUNICATIONS

TACT

- [ ] Failure to recognize differences in position between writer and receiver
- [ ] Impolitic tone — too brusk, argumentative, or insulting

SUPPORTING DETAIL

- [ ] Inadequate support for statements
- [ ] Too much undigested detail for busy superior

OPINION

- [ ] Adequate research but too great an intrusion of opinions
- [ ] Too few facts (and too little research) to entitle drawing of conclusions
- [ ] Presence of unasked for but clearly implied recommendations

ATTITUDE

- [ ] Too obvious a desire to please superior
- [ ] Too defensive in face of authority
- [ ] Too fearful of superior to be able to do best work

B. DOWNWARD COMMUNICATIONS

DIPLOMACY

- [ ] Overbearing attitude toward subordinates
- [ ] Insulting and/or personal references
- [ ] Unmindfulness that messages are representative of management group or even of company

CLARIFICATION OF DESIRES

- [ ] Confused, vague instructions
- [ ] Superior is not sure of what is wanted
- [ ] Withholding of information necessary to job at hand

MOTIVATIONAL ASPECTS

- [ ] Orders of superior seem arbitrary
- [ ] Superior's communications are manipulative and seemingly insincere

4. THOUGHT

PREPARATION

- [ ] Inadequate thought given to purpose of communication prior to its final completion
- [ ] Inadequate preparation or use of data known to be available

COMPETENCE

- [ ] Subject beyond intellectual capabilities of writer
- [ ] Subject beyond experience of writer

FIDELITY TO ASSIGNMENT

- [ ] Failure to stick to job assigned
- [ ] Too much made of routine assignment
- [ ] Too little made of assignment

ANALYSIS

- [ ] Superficial examination of data leading to unconscious overlooking of important pieces of evidence
- [ ] Failure to draw obvious conclusions from data presented
- [ ] Presentation of conclusions unjustified by evidence
- [ ] Failure to qualify tenuous assertions
- [ ] Failure to identify and justify assumptions used
- [ ] Bias, conscious or unconscious, which leads to distorted interpretation of data

PERSUASIVENESS

- [ ] Seems more convincing than facts warrant
- [ ] Seems less convincing than facts warrant
- [ ] Too obvious an attempt to sell ideas
- [ ] Lacks action-orientation and managerial viewpoint
- [ ] Too blunt an approach where subtlety and finesse called for

old grammar book rule would be especially wise to hark back to, and that is the topic sentence. Not only does placing a topic sentence at the beginning of each paragraph make it easier for the reader to grasp the content of the communication quickly; it also serves to discipline the writer into including only one main idea in each paragraph. Naturally, when a discussion of one idea means the expenditure of hundreds (or thousands) of words, paragraphs should be divided according to subdivisions of the main idea. In fact, an almost arbitrary division of paragraphs into units of four or five sentences is usually welcomed by the reader.

As for jargon, the only people who complain about it seriously are those who do not understand it. Moreover, it is fashionable for experts in a particular field to complain about their colleagues' use of jargon, but then to turn right around and use it themselves. The reason is that jargon is no more than shop talk. And when the person being addressed fully understands this private language, it is much more economical to use it than to go through laborious explanations of every idea that could be communicated in the shorthand of jargon. Naturally, when a writer knows that his message is going to be read by persons who are not familiar with the private language of his trade, he should be sure to translate as much of the jargon as he can into common terms.

The same thing holds true for simplicity of language. Simplicity is, I would think, always a "good." True, there is something lost from our language when interesting but unfamiliar words are no longer used. But isn't it true that the shrines in which these antiquities should be preserved lie in the domain of poetry or the novel, and not in business communications — which, after all, are not baroque cathedrals but functional edifices by which a job can be done?

The simplest way to say it, then, is invariably the best in business writing. But this fact the young executive does not always understand. Often he is eager to parade his vocabulary before his superiors, for fear his boss (who has never let him know that he admires simplicity, and may indeed adopt a pretentious and ponderous style himself) may think less of him.

Leading the Reader

But perhaps the most important aspect of readability is the one listed under the subtopic "reader direction." The failure of writers to seize their reader by the nose and lead him carefully through the intricacies of his communication is like an epidemic. The job that the writer must do is to develop the "skeleton" of the document that he is preparing. And, at the very beginning of his communication, he should identify the skeletal structure of his paper; he should, in effect, frame the discussion which is to follow.

You will see many of these frames at the beginning of articles published in HBR, where the editors take great pains to tell the reader quickly what the article is about and what specific areas will come under discussion during its progress. In every business document this initial frame, this statement of purpose and direction, should appear. Furthermore, in lengthy reports there should be many such frames; indeed, most major sections of business reports should begin with a new frame.

There should also be clear transitions between paragraphs. The goal should be that of having each element in a written message bear a close relationship to those elements which have preceded and those which follow it. Frequently a section should end with a brief summary, plus a sentence or two telling the reader the new direction of the article. These rather mechanical signposts, while frequently the bane of literary stylists, are always of valuable assistance to readers.

The final aspect of readability is the category that I call "focus." This term refers to the fact that many communications seem diffuse and out of focus, much like a picture on a television screen when the antennas are not properly directed. Sometimes in a report it seems as if one report has been superimposed on another, and that there are no clear and particular points the writer is trying to make. Thus the burden is put on the reader to ferret out the truly important points from the chaos.

If a writer wants to improve the readability of his writing, he must make sure that he has thought things through sufficiently, so that he can focus his readers' attention on the salient points.

Correctness

The one thing that flies to a writer's mind when he is told he cannot write is *correctness*. He immediately starts looking for grammar and punctuation mistakes in things that he has written.

But mistakes like these are hardly the most important aspects of business writing. The majority of executives are reasonably well educated and can, with a minimum of effort, make themselves adequately proficient in the "mechanics" of writing. Furthermore, as a man rises in his company, his typing (at least) will be done by a secretary, who can (and should) take the blame if a report is poorly punctuated and incorrect in grammar, not to mention being presented in an improper "format."

Then what is the most important point? Frequently, the insecure writer allows small mistakes in grammar and punctuation to become greatly magnified, and regards them as reflections on his education and, indeed, his social acceptability. A careless use of "he don't" may seem to be as large a disgrace in his mind as if he attended the company banquet in his shorts. And in some cases this is true. But he should also realize (as EXHIBIT II shows) that the ability to write *correctly* is not synonymous with the ability to write *well*. Hence, everyone should make sure that he does not become satisfied with the rather trivial act of mastering punctuation and grammar.

It is true, of course, that, in some instances, the inability to write correctly will cause a lack of clarity. We can all think of examples where a misplaced comma has caused serious confusion — although such instances, except in contracts and other legal documents, are fortunately rather rare.

A far more important aspect of correctness is "coherence." Coherence means the proper positioning of elements within a piece of writing so that it can be read clearly and sensibly. Take one example:

▼ *Incoherent:* "I think it will rain. However, no clouds are showing yet. Therefore, I will take my umbrella."

▲ *Coherent:* "Although no clouds are showing, I think it will rain. Therefore, I will take my umbrella."

Once a person has mastered the art of placing related words and sentences as close as possible to each other, he will be amazed at how smooth his formerly awkward writing becomes. But that is just the beginning. He will still have to make sure that he has placed paragraphs which are related in thought next to one an-

other, so that the ideas presented do not have to leapfrog over any intervening digressions.

Appropriateness

I have divided the category *appropriateness* into two sections reflecting the two main types of internal business communications — those going upward in the organization and those going downward. This distinction is one that cannot be found in textbooks on writing, although the ideas included here are commonplace in the human relations area.

There is an obvious difference between the type of communication that a boss writes to his subordinate and the type that the subordinate can get away with when he writes to his boss (or even the type that he drafts for his boss's signature). I suspect that many managers who have had their writing criticized had this unpleasant experience simply because of their failure to recognize the fact that messages are affected by the relative positions of the writer and the recipient in the organizational hierarchy.

Upward Communications

Let us roughly follow the order of the subtopics included under upward communications in EXHIBIT II. "Tact" is important. If a subordinate fails to recognize his role and writes in an argumentative or insulting tone, he is almost certain to reap trouble for himself (or for his boss if the document goes up under the boss's actual or implied signature). One of the perennially difficult problems facing any subordinate is how to tell a superior he is wrong. If the subordinate were the boss, most likely he *could* call a spade a spade; but since he is not, he has problems. And, in today's business world, bosses themselves spend much time figuring out how to handle problem communications with discretion. Often tender topics are best handled orally rather than in writing.

Two other subtopics — "supporting detail" and "opinion" — also require a distinction according to the writer's role. Since the communication is going upward, the writer will probably find it advisable to support his statements with considerable detail. On the other hand, he may run afoul of superiors who will be impatient if he gives too much detail and not enough generalization. Here is a classic instance where a word from above as to the amount of detail required in a particular assignment would be of inestimable value to the subordinate.

The same holds true for "opinion." In some cases, the subordinate may be criticized for introducing too many of his personal opinions — in fact, often for giving any recommendation at all. If the superior wishes the subordinate to make recommendations and to offer his own opinions, the burden is on the superior to tell him. If the superior fails to do so, the writer can at least try to make it clear where facts cease and opinions begin; then the superior can draw his own conclusions.

The writer's "attitude" is another important factor in upward communications. When a subordinate writes to his boss, it is almost impossible for him to communicate with the blandness that he might use if he were writing a letter to a friend. There may be many little things that he is doing throughout his writing that indicate either too great a desire to impress the boss or an insecurity which imparts a feeling of fearfulness, defensiveness, or truculence in the face of authority.

Downward Communications

While the subordinate who writes upward in the organization must use "tact," the boss who writes down to his subordinates must use "diplomacy." If he is overbearing or insulting (even without meaning to be), he will find his effectiveness as a manager severely limited. Furthermore, it is the foolish manager who forgets that, when he communicates downward, he speaks as a representative of management or even of the entire company. Careless messages have often played an important part in strikes and other corporate human relations problems.

It is also important for the superior to make sure that he has clarified in his own mind just what it is he wishes to accomplish. If he does not, he may give confused or vague instructions. (In this event, it is unfair for him to blame a subordinate for presenting a poorly focused document in return.) Another requirement is that the superior must make sure that he has supplied any information which the subordinate needs but could not be expected to know, and that he has sufficiently explained any points which may be misleading.

Motivation is important, too. When a superior gives orders, he will find that over the long run he will not be able to rely on mere power to force compliance with his requests. It seems typically American for a subordinate to resent and resist what he considers to be arbitrary decisions made for unknown reasons. If at all possible, the superior not only should explain the reasons why he gives an order but should point out (if he can) why his decision can be interpreted as being in the best interests of those whom it affects.

I am not, however, suggesting farfetched explanations of future benefits. In the long run, those can have a boomerang effect. Straight talk, carefully and tactfully couched, is the only sensible policy. If, for example, a subordinate's request for a new assignment has been denied because he needs further experience in his present assignment, he should be told the facts. Then, if it is also true that getting more experience may prepare him for a better position in the future, there is no reason why this information should not be included to "buffer" the impact of the refusal of a new assignment.

Thought

Here — a most important area — the superior has a tremendous vested interest in the reporting done by his subordinates. There is no substitute for the thought content of a communication. What good is accomplished if a message is excellent in all the other respects we have discussed — if it is readable, correct, and appropriate — yet the content is faulty? It can even do harm if the other aspects succeed in disguising the fact that it is superficial, stupid, or biased. The superior receiving it may send it up through the organization with his signature, or, equally serious, he may make an important (and disastrous) decision based on it.

Here is the real *guts* of business writing — intelligent content, something most purveyors of business writing gimmicks conveniently forget. It is also something that most training programs shortchange. The discipline of translating thoughts into words and organizing these thoughts logically has no equal as intellectual training. For there is one slogan that is true: "Disorganized, illogical writing reflects a disorganized, illogical (and untrained) mind."

That is why the first topic in this section is "preparation." Much disorganized writing results from insufficient preparation, from a failure to think through and isolate the purpose and the aim of the writing job. Most writers tend to think as they write; in fact, most of us do not even know what it is we think until we have actually written it down. The inescapability of making a well-thought-out outline before dictating seems obvious.

A primary aspect of *thought,* consequently, is the intellectual "competence" of the writer. If a report is bad merely because the subject is far beyond the experience of the writer, it is not his fault. Thus his superior should be able to reject the analysis and at the same time accept the blame for having given his assistant a job that he simply could not do. But what about the many cases where the limiting factor *is* basically the intellectual capacity of the writer? It is foolish to tell a man that he cannot *write* if in effect he simply does not have the intellectual ability to do the job that has been assigned to him.

Another aspect of thought is "fidelity to the assignment." Obviously the finest performance in the world on a topic other than the one assigned is fruitless, but such violent distortions of the assignment fortunately are rare. Not so rare, unfortunately, are reports which subtly miss the point, or wander away from it. Any consistent tendency on the part of the writer to drag in his pet remedies or favorite villains should be pointed out quickly, as should persistent efforts to grind personal axes.

Another lapse of "fidelity" is far more forgivable. This occurs when an eager subordinate tends to make too much of a routine assignment and consistently turns memos into 50-page reports. On the other hand, some subordinates may consistently make too little of an assignment and tend to do superficial and poorly researched pieces of work.

Perhaps the most important aspect of thought is the component "analysis." Here is where the highly intelligent are separated from those less gifted, and those who will dig from those who content themselves with superficial work. Often subordinates who have not had the benefit of experience under a strict taskmaster (either in school or on the job) are at a loss to understand why their reports are considered less than highly effective. Such writers, for example, may fail to draw obvious conclusions from the data that they have presented. On the other hand, they may offer conclusions which are seemingly unjustified by the evidence contained in their reports.

Another difficulty is that many young managers (and old ones, too) are unsophisticated in their appreciation of just what constitutes evidence. For example, if they base an entire report on the fact that sales are going to go up the next year simply because one assistant sales manager thinks so, they should expect to have their conclusions thrown out of court. They may also find themselves in difficulty if they fail to identify and justify assumptions which have been forced on them by the absence of factual data. Assumptions, of course, are absolutely necessary in this world of imperfect knowledge — especially when we deal with future developments — but it is the writer's responsibility to point out that certain assumptions have been made and that the validity of his analysis depends on whether or not these assumptions prove to be justified.

Another serious error in "analysis" is that of bias. Few superiors will respect a communication which is consciously or unconsciously biased. A writer who is incapable of making an objective analysis of all sides of a question, or of all alternatives to action, will certainly find his path to the top to be a dead end. On the other hand, especially in many younger writers, bias enters unconsciously, and it is only by a patient identification of the bias that the superior will be able to help the subordinate develop a truly objective analytical ability.

Persuasiveness

This discussion of bias in reporting raises the question of "persuasiveness." "Every letter is a sales letter of some sort," goes the refrain. And it is true that persuasiveness in writing can range from the "con man" type of presentation to that which results from a happy blending of the four elements of business writing I have described. While it would be naive to suggest that it is not often necessary for executives to write things in manipulative ways to achieve their ends *in the short run,* it would be foolish to imply that this type of writing will be very effective with the same people (if they are reasonably intelligent) *over the long run.* Understandably, therefore, the "con man" approach will not be particularly effective in the large business organization.

On the other hand, persuasiveness is a necessary aspect of organizational writing. Yet it is difficult to describe the qualities which serve to make a communication persuasive. It could be a certain ring of conviction about the way recommendations are advanced; it could be enthusiasm, or an understanding of the reader's desires, and a playing up to them. One can persuade by hitting with the blunt edge of the axe or by cutting finely with the sharp edge to prepare the way. Persuasion could result from a fine sense of discretion, of hinting but not stating overtly things which are impolitic to mention; or it could result from an action-orientation that conveys top management's desire for results rather than a more philosophical approach to a subject. In fact, it could be many things.

In an organization, the best test to apply for the propriety of persuasiveness is to ask yourself whether you would care to take action on the basis of what your own communication presents. In the long run, it is dangerous to assume that everyone else is stupid and malleable; so, if you would be offended or damaged in the event that you were persuaded to take the action suggested, you should restate the communication. This test eliminates needless worry about slightly dishonest but well-meaning letters of congratulation, or routine progress reports written merely for a filing record, and the like. But it does bring into sharp focus those messages that cross the line from persuasiveness to bias;

these are the ones that will injure others and so eventually injure you.

Conclusion

No one can honestly estimate the billions of dollars that are spent in U.S. industry on written communications, but the amount must be staggering. By contrast, the amount of thinking and effort that goes into improving the effectiveness of business writing is tiny — a mouse invading a continent. A written performance inventory (like Exhibit ii) in itself is not the answer. But a checklist of writing elements should enable executives to speak about writing in a common tongue and hence be a vehicle by which individual and group improvement in writing can take place.

By executives' own vote, no aspect of a manager's performance is of greater importance to his success than communication, particularly written communication. By the facts, however, no part of business practice receives less formal and intelligent attention. What this article asserts is that when an individual asks, "What do you mean I can't write?" — and has every desire to improve — his company owes him a sensible and concrete answer.

THE purpose of communication is persuasion." I heard this aphorism in one of those management improvement sessions (at a resort hotel) that the contemporary corporation uses so extensively, to "improve communications" among other reasons. It has haunted me ever since. For what it says is that there is no point in mere transfer of cognitive knowledge of information, no point in journalistic or scientific reporting. Communication becomes a strategy of power, a model of "winning friends and influencing people." Its enemy is not misunderstanding or ignorance but improper attitudes and values.

If this point is grasped, the managerial enthusiasm for "good communications" becomes more understandable if not more lovable. The goal is shared values, but perhaps not shared information. Indeed, completely shared information, including information on what the communicators aim to accomplish, might well defeat the "appeals to reason" that are really appeals to sentiments.

Wilbert E. Moore, *The Conduct of the Corporation*
New York, Random House, 1962, pp. 72–73.

Marvin H. Swift

Clear writing means clear thinking means . . .

Saying what we mean and meaning what we say must be in harmony for good communication

Foreword

Very few people have the ability to write effortlessly and perfectly; most of us must sweat over the process of revision, drafting, and redrafting until we get it right. Equally, very few people think accurately enough so that mere transcriptions of "what they have in mind" can serve as intelligent communications. Here the author points out that we tend to revise our words and refine our thoughts simultaneously; the improvements we make in our thinking and the improvements we make in our style reinforce each other, and they cannot be divorced. His analysis of the way in which a manager reworks and rethinks a memo of minor importance points up a constant management challenge of major importance—the clear and accurate expression of a well-focused message.

Mr. Swift is Associate Professor of Communication at the General Motors Institute, where he has taught in a variety of programs since 1951.

If you are a manager, you constantly face the problem of putting words on paper. If you are like most managers, this is not the sort of problem you enjoy. It is hard to do, and time consuming; and the task is doubly difficult when, as is usually the case, your words must be designed to change the behavior of others in the organization.

But the chore is there and must be done. How? Let's take a specific case.

Let's suppose that everyone at X Corporation, from the janitor on up to the chairman of the board, is using the office copiers for personal matters; income tax forms, church programs, children's term papers, and God knows what else are being duplicated by the gross. This minor piracy costs the company a pretty penny, both directly and in employee time, and the general manager—let's call him Sam Edwards—decides the time has come to lower the boom.

Sam lets fly by dictating the following memo to his secretary:

```
To: All Employees
From: Samuel Edwards, General Manager
Subject: Abuse of Copiers

It has recently been brought to my attention
that many of the people who are employed by
this company have taken advantage of their
positions by availing themselves of the
copiers. More specifically, these machines
are being used for other than company
business.

Obviously, such practice is contrary to
company policy and must cease and desist
immediately. I wish therefore to inform all
concerned -- those who have abused policy or
will be abusing it -- that their behavior
cannot and will not be tolerated. Accord-
ingly, anyone in the future who is unable to
control himself will have his employment
terminated.

If there are any questions about company
policy, please feel free to contact this
office.
```

Now the memo is on his desk for his signature. He looks it over; and the more he looks, the worse it reads. In fact, it's lousy. So he revises it three times, until it finally is in the form that follows:

To: All Employees

From: Samuel Edwards, General Manager

Subject: Use of Copiers

We are revamping our policy on the use of copiers for personal matters. In the past we have not encouraged personnel to use them for such purposes because of the costs involved. But we also recognize, perhaps belatedly, that we can solve the problem if each of us pays for what he takes.

We are therefore putting these copiers on a pay-as-you-go basis. The details are simple enough ....

Samuel Edwards

This time Sam thinks the memo looks good, and it *is* good. Not only is the writing much improved, but the problem should now be solved. He therefore signs the memo, turns it over to his secretary for distribution, and goes back to other things.

From verbiage to intent

I can only speculate on what occurs in a writer's mind as he moves from a poor draft to a good revision, but it is clear that Sam went through several specific steps, mentally as well as physically, before he had created his end product:

○ He eliminated wordiness.
○ He modulated the tone of the memo.
○ He revised the policy it stated.

Let's retrace his thinking through each of these processes.

Eliminating wordiness

Sam's basic message is that employees are not to use the copiers for their own affairs at company expense. As he looks over his first draft, however, it seems so long that this simple message has become diffused. With the idea of trimming the memo down, he takes another look at his first paragraph:

It has recently been brought to my attention that many of the people who are employed by this company have taken advantage of their positions by availing themselves of the copiers. More specifically, these machines are being used for other than company business.

He edits it like this:

Item: "recently"
Comment to himself: Of course; else why write about the problem? So delete the word.

Item: "It has been brought to my attention"
Comment: Naturally. Delete it.

Item: "the people who are employed by this company"
Comment: Assumed. Why not just "employees"?

Item: "by availing themselves" and "for other than company business"
Comment: Since the second sentence repeats the first, why not coalesce?

And he comes up with this:

Employees have been using the copiers for personal matters.

He proceeds to the second paragraph. More confident of himself, he moves in broader swoops, so that the deletion process looks like this:

Obviously, such practice is contrary to company policy and ~~must cease and desist immediately. I wish therefore to inform all concerned — those who have abused policy or will be abusing it — that their behavior cannot and will not be tolerated. Accordingly, anyone in the future who is unable to control himself will have his employment terminated.~~  will result in dismissal.

The final paragraph, apart from "company policy" and "feel free," looks all right, so the total memo now reads as follows:

To: All Employees

From: Samuel Edwards, General Manager

Subject: Abuse of Copiers

Employees have been using the copiers for personal matters. Obviously, such practice is contrary to company policy and will result in dismissal.

If there are any questions, please contact this office.

Sam now examines his efforts by putting these questions to himself:

Question: Is the memo free of deadwood?

Answer: Very much so. In fact, it's good, tight prose.

Question: Is the policy stated?

Answer: Yes—sharp and clear.

Question: Will the memo achieve its intended purpose?

Answer: Yes. But it sounds foolish.

Question: Why?

Answer: The wording is too harsh; I'm not going to fire anybody over this.

Question: How should I tone the thing down?

To answer this last question, Sam takes another look at the memo.

Correcting the tone

What strikes his eye as he looks it over? Perhaps these three words:

○ Abuse . . .

○ Obviously . . .

○ . . . dismissal . . .

The first one is easy enough to correct: he substitutes "use" for "abuse." But "obviously" poses a problem and calls for reflection. If the policy is obvious, why are the copiers being used? Is it that people are outrightly dishonest? Probably not. But that implies the policy isn't obvious; and whose fault is this? Who neglected to clarify policy? And why "dismissal" for something never publicized?

These questions impel him to revise the memo once again:

```
To: All Employees
From: Samuel Edwards, General Manager
Subject: Use of Copiers

Copiers are not to be used for personal
matters. If there are any questions,
please contact this office.
```

Revising the policy itself

The memo now seems courteous enough—at least it is not discourteous—but it is just a blank, perhaps overly simple, statement of policy. Has he really thought through the policy itself?

Reflecting on this, Sam realizes that some people will continue to use the copiers for personal business anyhow. If he seriously intends to enforce the basic policy (first sentence), he will have to police the equipment, and that raises the question of costs all over again.

Also, the memo states that he will maintain an open-door policy (second sentence)—and surely there will be some, probably a good many, who will stroll in and offer to pay for what they use. His secretary has enough to do without keeping track of affairs of that kind.

Finally, the first and second sentences are at odds with each other. The first says that personal copying is out, and the second implies that it can be arranged.

The facts of organizational life thus force Sam to clarify in his own mind exactly what his position on the use of copiers is going to be. As he sees the problem now, what he really wants to do is put the copiers on a pay-as-you-go basis. After making that decision, he begins anew:

```
To: All Employees
From: Samuel Edwards, General Manager
Subject: Use of copiers

We are revamping our policy on the use of
copiers . . . . . . .
```

This is the draft that goes into distribution and now allows him to turn his attention to other problems.

The chicken or the egg?

What are we to make of all this? It seems a rather lengthy and tedious report of what, after all, is a routine writing task created by a problem of minor importance. In making this kind of analysis, have I simply labored the obvious?

To answer this question, let's drop back to the original draft. If you read it over, you will see that Sam began with this kind of thinking:

○ "The employees are taking advantage of the company."

○ "I'm a nice guy, but now I'm going to play Dutch uncle."

∴ "I'll write them a memo that tells them to shape up or ship out."

In his final version, however, his thinking is quite different:

○ "Actually, the employees are pretty mature, responsible people. They're capable of understanding a problem."

○ "Company policy itself has never been crystallized. In fact, this is the first memo on the subject."

○ "I don't want to overdo this thing—any employee can make an error in judgment."

∴ "I'll set a reasonable policy and write a memo that explains how it ought to operate."

Sam obviously gained a lot of ground between the first draft and the final version, and this implies two things. First, if a manager is to write effectively, he needs to isolate and define, as fully as possible, all the critical variables in the writing process and scrutinize what he writes for its clarity, simplicity, tone, and the rest. Second, after he has clarified his thoughts on paper, he may find that what he has written is not what has to be said. In this sense, writing is feedback and a way for the manager to discover himself. What are his real attitudes toward that amorphous, undifferentiated gray mass of employees "out there"? Writing is a way of finding out. By objectifying his thoughts in the medium of language, he gets a chance to see what is going on in his mind.

In other words, *if the manager writes well, he will think well.* Equally, the more clearly he has thought out his message before he starts to dictate, the more likely he is to get it right on paper the first time round. In other words, *if he thinks well, he will write well.*

Hence we have a chicken-and-the-egg situation: writing and thinking go hand in hand; and when one is good, the other is likely to be good.

Revision sharpens thinking

More particularly, rewriting is the key to improved thinking. It demands a real openmindedness and objectivity. It demands a willingness to cull verbiage so that ideas stand out clearly. And it demands a willingness to meet logical contradictions head on and trace them to the premises that have created them. In short, it forces a writer to get up his courage and expose his thinking process to his own intelligence.

Obviously, revising is hard work. It demands that you put yourself through the wringer, intellectually and emotionally, to squeeze out the best you can offer. Is it worth the effort? Yes, it is—if you believe you have a responsibility to think and communicate effectively.

The rewards of successful communication

Good communications writing pays its author in both satisfactions and success. Its rewards far outweigh its achievement costs.

But rewards accrue only after effort has become a habit. Good communications writing is five-tenths mental discipline, four-tenths willingness to rework first drafts, and one-tenth aptitude.

Secondary are the direct returns from readers. Most important are the rewards manifested in improved ability to use your mind effectively. These result from practice of the mental disciplines required for good communications writing.

Establishing both objective and purpose before writing, for example, gives practice in using procedures needed to solve any problem. Considering your reader's needs and desires is a habit readily convertible to any human relations. Exorcising self-centeredness is a good routine to establish.

Bringing to focus the main idea of each communication makes one adept in taking decision making's first and most vital step. Habitually reworking first drafts routinizes a . . . practice often useful in the business of living.

No way to creative mental habits is so open to so many people as good communications writing. Its intangible rewards are inevitable by-products of acquiring the ability to communicate well in writing.

To gain these waiting rewards, however, one has to discipline, but not limit, his thinking. He has to make a habit of thinking before he acts— not only before he writes. Regularly, he must do plain hard work (editing and rewriting) to lift his every communication to the standard his sound thinking has set.

There is no other way. Good communications writing is work. But it is rewarding work—if you persevere in doing it well.

Norman G. Shidle,
The Art of Successful Communication,
New York, McGraw-Hill Book
Company, 1965, pp. 258-259.

John S. Fielden

What you say in a letter or a memorandum is partly how you say it. Your message – your real intentions – can get lost in your words. Seeing the whole message a communication can convey is more than understanding the dictionary definitions of the words you choose. It is also discerning the intentions and emphases and relationships reflected in the connotations of those words and the sentence structures you use. Writing an effective letter is far more than stating the basic message you wish to give to someone. It is also conveying how you wish to relate to the recipient and what you want him or her to feel in response. And that's important because it may determine what the reader does about the message.

You convey these additional meanings through the style you choose to write with. There is no single style for all occasions. Sometimes it's tactful to be personal, and sometimes it's best to be fairly impersonal. At times it feels right to be simple and direct, and at other times roundabout and colorful. Sometimes you just need to be forceful. One thing is sure: strategy is part of style. The message you want to send is partly in your tone. Any message varies according to the way you phrase it.

The author, who has taught classes in business writing for many years, describes six styles that you will find appropriate for various writing situations in business.

Mr. Fielden is University Professor of Management Communication at the University of Alabama. He has been an associate editor at HBR and dean of the business schools at Boston University and the University of Alabama. As managing partner of Fielden Associates, he has consulted on management communication with many of the nation's leading corporations. This is the seventh article he has written for HBR. One of them – "What Do You Mean I Can't Write?" (May-June 1964) – has been one of HBR's ten most popular reprints.

Illustrations by Geoffrey Moss.

'What do you mean you don't like my style?'

To get your message across, vary your writing style to suit each situation you have to deal with.

In large corporations all over the country, people are playing a game of paddleball – with drafts of letters instead of balls. Volley after volley goes back and forth between those who sign the letters and those who actually write them. It's a game nobody likes, but it continues, and we pay for it. The workday has no extra time for such unproductiveness. What causes this round robin of revision?

Typos? Factual misstatements? Poor format? No. *Style* does. Ask yourself how often you hear statements like these:

☐ "It takes new assistants about a year to learn my style. Until they do, I have no choice but to bounce letters back for revision. I won't sign a letter if it doesn't sound like me."

☐ "I find it difficult, almost impossible, to write letters for my boss's signature. The boss's style is different from mine."

In companies where managers primarily write their own letters, confusion about style also reigns. Someone sends out a letter and hears later that the reaction was not at all the one desired. It is reported that the reader doesn't like the writer's "tone." A colleague looks over a copy of the letter and says, "No wonder the reader doesn't like this letter. You shouldn't have said things the way you did. You used the wrong style for a letter like this." "Style?" the writer says. "What's wrong with my style?" "I don't know" is the response. "I just don't like the way you said things."

Everybody talks about style, but almost nobody understands the meaning of the word in the business environment. And this lack of understanding hurts both those who write letters for another's signature and those who write for themselves. Neither knows where to turn for help. Strunk and White's marvelous book *The Elements of Style* devotes only a few pages to a discussion of style, and that concerns only literary style.[1] Books like the Chicago *Manual of Style*[2] seem to define style as all the technical points they cover, from abbreviations and capitalizations to footnotes and bibliographies. And dictionary definitions are usually too vague to be helpful.

Even such a general definition as this offers scant help, although perhaps it comes closest to how business people use the word:

> Style is "the way something is said or done, as distinguished from its substance."[3]

Managers signing drafts written by subordinates, and the subordinates themselves, already know that they have trouble agreeing on "the way things should be said." What, for instance, is meant by "way"? In trying to find that way, both managers and subordinates are chasing a will-o'-the-wisp. There *is* no magical way, no perfect, universal way of writing things that will fend off criticism of style. There is no one style of writing in business that is appropriate in all situations and for all readers, even though managers and subordinates usually talk and behave as if there were.

But why all the confusion? Isn't style really the way we say things? Certainly it is. Then writing style must be made up of the particular words we select to express our ideas and the types of sentences and paragraphs we put together to convey those ideas. What else could it be? Writing has no tone of voice or body gesture to impart additional meanings. In written communication, tone comes from what a reader reads into the words and sentences used.

Words express more than *denotations*, the definitions found in dictionaries. They also carry *connotations*. In the feelings and images associated with each word lies the capacity a writing style has for producing an emotional reaction in a reader. And in that capacity lies the tone of a piece of writing. Style is largely a matter of tone. The writer uses a style; the reader infers a communication's tone. Tone comes from what a reader reads into the words and sentences a writer uses.

In the business environment, tone is especially important. Business writing is not literary writing. Literary artists use unique styles to "express" themselves to a general audience. Business people write to particular persons in particular situations, not so much to express themselves as to accomplish particular purposes, "to get a job done." If a reader doesn't like a novelist's tone, nothing much can happen to the writer short of failing to sell some books. In the business situation, however, an offensive style may not only prevent a sale but may also turn away a customer, work against a promotion, or even cost you a job.

While style can be distinguished from substance, it cannot be divorced from substance. In business writing, style cannot be divorced from the circumstances under which something is written or from the likes, dislikes, position, and power of the reader.

A workable definition of style
in business writing would be something like this:
Style is that choice of words, sentences, and paragraph format which by virtue of being appropriate to the situation and to the power positions of both writer and reader produces the desired reaction and result.

Which style is yours?

Let's take a case and see what we can learn from it. Assume that you are an executive in a very large information-processing company. You receive the following letter:

Mr.(Ms.) Leslie J. Cash
XYZ Corporation
Main Street
Anytown, U.S.A.

Dear Leslie:
As you know, I respect your professional opinion highly. The advice your people have given us at ABC Corporation as we have moved into a comprehensive information system over the past three years has been very helpful. I'm writing to you now, however, in my

1 William Strunk, Jr. and E.B. White, *The Elements of Style* (New York: Macmillan, 1979).

2 *A Manual of Style* (Chicago: University of Chicago Press, 1969).

3 *The American Heritage Dictionary of the English Language* (Boston: American Heritage and Houghton Mifflin, 1969).

role as chairman of the executive committee of the trustees of our hospital. We at Community General Hospital have decided to establish a skilled volunteer data processing evaluation team to assess proposals to automate our hospital's information flow.

I have suggested your name to my committee. I know you could get real satisfaction from helping your community as a member of this evaluation team. Please say yes. I look forward to being able to count on your advice. Let me hear from you soon.

Frank J. Scalpel
Chairman
Executive Committee
Community General Hospital
Anytown, U.S.A.

If you accepted the appointment mentioned in this letter, you would have a conflict of interest. You are an executive at XYZ, Inc. You know that XYZ will submit a proposal to install a comprehensive information system for the hospital. Mr. Scalpel is the vice president of finance at ABC Corp., a very good customer of yours. You know him well since you have worked with him on community programs as well as in the business world.

I can think of four typical responses to Scalpel's letter. Each says essentially the same thing, but each is written in a different business style:

Response 1

Mr. Frank J. Scalpel
Chairman, Executive Committee
Community General Hospital
Anytown, U.S.A.

Dear Frank,
As you realize, this litigious age often makes it necessary for large companies to take stringent measures not only to avoid conflicts of interest on the part of their employees but also to preclude even the very suggestion of conflict. And, since my company intends to submit a proposal with reference to automating the hospital's information flow, it would not appear seemly for me to be part of an evaluation team assessing

competitors' proposals. Even if I were to excuse myself from consideration of the XYZ proposal, I would still be vulnerable to charges that I gave short shrift to competitors' offerings.

If there is any other way that I can serve the committee that will not raise this conflict-of-interest specter, you know that I would find it pleasurable to be of service, as always.

Sincerely,

Response 2

Dear Frank,
Your comments relative to your respect for my professional opinion are most appreciated. Moreover, your invitation to serve on the hospital's data processing evaluation team is received with gratitude, albeit with some concern.

The evaluation team must be composed of persons free of alliance with any of the vendors submitting proposals. For that reason, it is felt that my services on the team could be construed as a conflict of interest.

Perhaps help can be given in some other way. Again, please be assured that your invitation has been appreciated.

Sincerely,

Response 3

Dear Frank,
Thank you for suggesting my name as a possible member of your data processing evaluation team. I wish I could serve, but I cannot.

XYZ intends, naturally, to submit a proposal to automate the hospital's information flow. You can see the position of conflict I would be in if I were on the evaluation team.

Just let me know of any other way I can be of help. You know I would be more than willing. Thanks again for the invitation.

Cordially,

Response 4

Dear Frank,
Thanks for the kind words and the invitation. Sure wish I could say yes. Can't, though.

XYZ intends to submit a sure-fire proposal on automating the hospital's information. Shouldn't be judge and advocate at the same time!

Any other way I can help, Frank — just ask. Thanks again.

Cordially,

What do you think of these letters?

Which letter has the style you like best? Check off the response you prefer.

Response   1   2   3   4
        ☐   ☐   ☐   ☐

Which letter has the style resembling the one you customarily use? Again, check off your choice.

Response   1   2   3   4
        ☐   ☐   ☐   ☐

Which terms best describe the style of each letter? Check the appropriate boxes.

Response 1	☐ Colorful ☐ Dull	☐ Passive ☐ Forceful	☐ Personal ☐ Impersonal
Response 2	☐ Colorful ☐ Dull	☐ Passive ☐ Forceful	☐ Personal ☐ Impersonal
Response 3	☐ Colorful ☐ Dull	☐ Passive ☐ Forceful	☐ Personal ☐ Impersonal
Response 4	☐ Colorful ☐ Dull	☐ Passive ☐ Forceful	☐ Personal ☐ Impersonal

---

Let's compare reactions

Now that you've given your reactions, let's compare them with some of mine.

Response 1 seems cold, impersonal, complex. Most business people would, I think, react somewhat negatively to this style because it seems to push the reader away from the writer. Its word choice has a cerebral quality that, while flattering to the reader's intelligence, also parades the writer's.

Response 2 is fairly cool, quite impersonal, and somewhat complex. Readers' reactions will probably be neither strongly positive nor strongly negative. This style of writing is "blah" because it is heavily passive. Instead of saying "I appreciate your comments," it says "Your comments are most appreciated"; instead of "I think that my services could be construed as a conflict of interest," it says "It is felt that my services could be construed...." The use of the passive voice subordinates writers modestly to the back of sentences or causes them to disappear.

This is the impersonal, passive style of writing that many with engineering, mathematics, or scientific backgrounds feel most comfortable using. It is harmless, but it is certainly not colorful; nor is it forceful or interesting.

Response 3 illustrates the style of writing that most high-level executives use. It is simple; it is personal; it is warm without being syrupy; it is forceful, like a firm handshake. Almost everybody in business likes this style, although lower-level managers often find themselves afraid to write so forthrightly (and, as a result, often find themselves retreating into the styles of responses 1 and 2 — the style of 1 to make themselves look "smart" to superiors and the style of 2 to appear unbossy and fairly impersonal). Persons who find response 2 congenial may feel a bit dubious about the appropriateness of response 3. (Although I have no way of proving this judgment, I would guess that more readers in high positions — perhaps more owner-managers — would like response 3 than would readers who are still in lower positions.)

Response 4 goes beyond being forceful; it is annoyingly self-confident and breezy. It is colorful and conversational to an extreme, and it is so intensely personal and warm that many business people would be offended, even if they were very close acquaintances of Frank Scalpel's. "It sounds like an advertising person's chitchat," some would probably say.

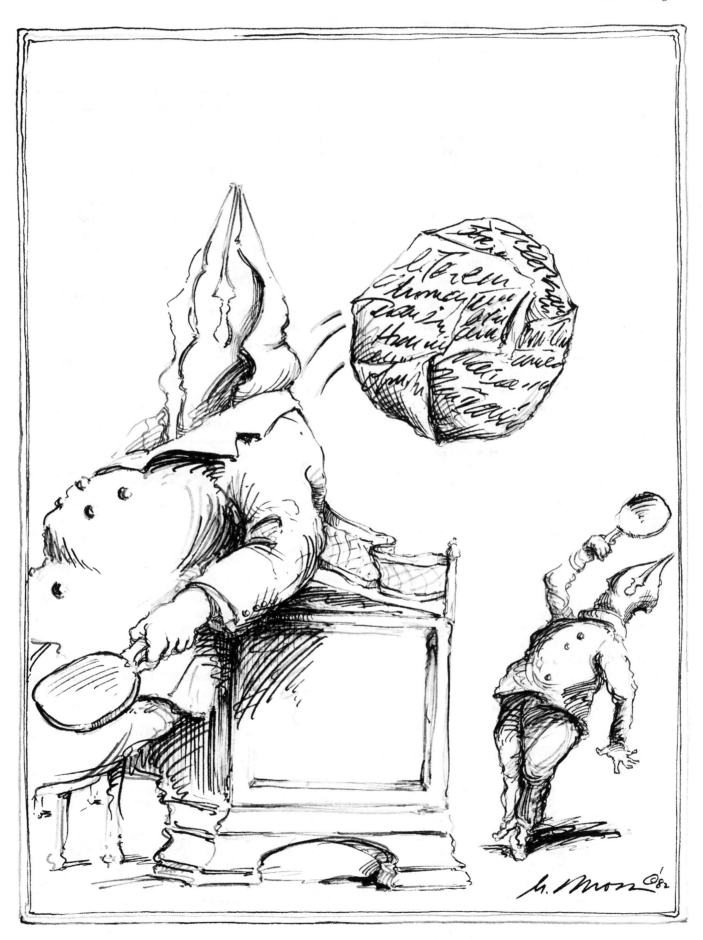

Strategy is part of style

As you compared your responses with mine, did you say, "What difference does it make which style *I* like or which most resembles *my* customary style? What matters is which style will go over best with Mr. Scalpel in this situation"? If you did, we're getting somewhere.

Earlier, when we defined business writing style, some may have wanted to add, "And that style should sound like me." This was left out for a good reason. Circumstances not only alter cases; they alter the "you" that it is wise for your style to project. Sometimes it's wise to be forceful; at other times it's suicidal. Sometimes being sprightly and colorful is appropriate; at other times it's ludicrous. There are times to be personal and times to be impersonal.

Not understanding this matter of style and tone is why the big corporation game of paddleball between managers and subordinates goes on and on. The subordinate tries to imitate the boss's style, but in actuality—unless the boss is extremely insensitive—he or she has no single style for all circumstances and for all readers. What usually happens is that after several tries, the subordinate writes a letter that the boss signs. "Aha!" the subordinate says. "So that's what the boss wants!" And then the subordinate tries to use that style for all situations and readers. Later, the superior begins rejecting drafts written in the very style he or she professed liking before. Both parties throw up their hands.

This volleying is foolish and wasteful. Both superior and subordinate have to recognize that in business writing, style cannot be considered apart from the given situation or from the person to whom the writing is directed. Expert writers select the style that fits a particular reader and the type of writing situation with which they are faced. In business, people often face the following writing situations:

Positive situations.
Saying yes or conveying good news.

Situations where some action is asked of the reader.
Giving orders or persuading someone to do as requested.

Information-conveying situations.
Giving the price of ten widgets, for example.

Negative situations.
Saying no or relaying bad news.

In each of these situations, the choice of style is of strategic importance.

In positive situations, a writer can relax on all fronts. Readers are usually so pleased to hear the good news that they pay little attention to anything else. Yet it is possible for someone to communicate good news in such a cold, impersonal, roundabout, and almost begrudging way that the reader becomes upset.

Action-request situations involve a form of bargaining. In a situation where the writer holds all the power, he or she can use a forceful commanding style. When the writer holds no power over the reader, though, actions have to be asked for and the reader persuaded, not ordered. In such cases, a forceful style will not be suitable at all.

In information-conveying situations, getting the message across forcefully and straightforwardly is best. Such situations are not usually charged emotionally.

In negative situations, diplomacy becomes very important. The right style depends on the relative positions of the person saying no and the person being told no.

For instance, if you were Leslie Cash, the person in the example at the beginning of the article whom Frank Scalpel was inviting to serve on a hospital's evaluation team, you would be in a situation of having to say no to a very important customer of your company. You would also be in a doubly sensitive situation because it is unlikely that Mr. Scalpel would fail to recognize that he is asking you to enter a conflict-of-interest situation. He is probably asking you *anyway.* Therefore, you would not only have to tell him no, but you would have to avoid telling him that he has asked you to do something that is highly unethical. In this instance, you would be faced with communicating two negative messages at once or else not giving Scalpel any sensible reason for refusing to serve.

Suit your style to the situation

Now that we've thought about the strategic implications of style, let's go back to look at each of the responses to Scalpel's request and ask ourselves which is best.

Do we *want* to be personal and warm? Usually yes. But in this situation? Do we want to communicate clearly and directly and forcefully? Usually yes. But here? Do we want to appear as if we're brushing aside the conflict, as the third response does? Or do we want to approach that issue long-windedly, as in

the first response, or passively, as in the second? What is the strategically appropriate style?

In the abstract, we have no way of knowing which of these responses will go over best with Mr. Scalpel. The choice is a matter of judgment in a concrete situation. Judging the situation accurately is what separates successful from unsuccessful executive communicators.

Looking at the situation with strategy in mind, we note that in the first response, the writer draws back from being close, knowing that it is necessary to reject not only one but two of the reader's requests. By using legalistic phraseology and Latinate vocabulary, the writer lowers the personal nature of the communication and transforms it into a formal statement. It gives an abstract, textbooklike response that removes the tone of personal rejection.

The very fact that response 1 is difficult to read and dull in impact may be a strategic asset in this type of negative situation. But if in this situation a subordinate presented response 1 to you for your signature, would it be appropriate for you to reject it because it is not written in the style *you* happen to *like* best in the abstract—say, the style of response 3?

Now let's look at response 2. Again, we see that a lack of personal warmth may be quite appropriate to the situation at hand. Almost immediately, the letter draws back into impersonality. And by using the passive constantly, the writer avoids the need to say "I must say no." Furthermore, the term *construed* reinforces the passive in the second paragraph. This term is a very weak but possibly a strategically wise way of implying that *some* persons (*other* people, not the writer) could interpret Scalpel's request as an invitation to participate in an improper action. Now we can see that, instead of seeming dull and lacking in personal warmth as it did in the abstract, response 2 may be the type of letter we would be wise to send out, that is, when we have taken the whole situation into careful consideration and not just our personal likes and dislikes.

The third response, and to even greater extent the fourth, have styles that are strategically inappropriate for this situation. In fact, Scalpel might well regard the colorful style of the fourth response as highly offensive. Both responses directly and forcefully point out the obvious conflict, but by being so direct each runs the risk of subtly offending him. (The third response is "you can see the position of conflict I'd be in if I were on the evaluation team," and the fourth is "Shouldn't be judge and advocate at the same time!") We could make a pretty strong argument that the direct, forceful, candid style of the third response and the breezy, warm, colorful, intensely personal "advertising" style of the fourth response may both prove ineffectual in a delicate, negative situation such as this.

What effect do you want?

At this point, readers may say, "All right. I'm convinced. I need to adjust my style to what is appropriate in each situation. And I also need to give directions to others to let them know how to adjust their styles. But I haven't the foggiest notion of how to do either!" Some suggestions for varying your writing style follow. I am not implying that a communication must be written in one style only. A letter to be read aloud at a colleague's retirement party, for instance, may call not only for a warm, personal style but for colorfulness as well. A long analytic report may require a passive, impersonal style, but the persuasive cover letter may call for recommendations being presented in a very forceful style.

For a forceful style

This style is usually appropriate only in situations where the writer has the power, such as in action requests in the form of orders or when you are saying no firmly but politely to a subordinate.

- [ ] Use the active voice. Have your sentences do something to people and to objects, not just lie there having things done to them; have them give orders: "Correct this error immediately" (you-understood is the subject) instead of "A correction should be made" (which leaves the reader wondering, made by whom).

- [ ] Step up front and be counted: "I have decided not to recommend you for promotion" instead of "Unfortunately, a positive recommendation for your promotion is not forthcoming."

- [ ] Do not beat around the bush or act like a politician. If something needs to be said, say it directly.

- [ ] Write most of your sentences in subject-verb-object order. Do not weaken them by putting namby-pamby phrases before the subject: "I have decided to fund your project" instead of "After much deliberation and weighing of the pros and cons, I have decided to fund your project."

☐ Do not weaken sentences by relegating the point or the action to a subordinate clause:
If your point is that your company has won a contract, say "Acme won the contract, although the bidding was intense and highly competitive," not "Although Acme won the contract, the bidding was intense and highly competitive."

☐ Adopt a tone of confidence and surety about what you say by avoiding weasel words like:
"Possibly," "maybe," "perhaps."
"It could be concluded that...."
"Some might conclude that...."

For a passive style

This style is often appropriate in negative situations and in situations where the writer is in a lower position than the reader.

☐ Avoid the imperative—never give an order:
Say "A more effective and time-conserving presentation of ideas should be devised before our next meeting" as opposed to "Do a better job of presenting your ideas at our next meeting. Respect my time and get right to the point."

☐ Use the passive voice heavily because it subordinates the subject to the end of the sentence or buries the subject entirely. The passive is especially handy when you are in a low-power position and need to convey negative information to a reader who is in a higher position (an important customer, for instance):
Say "Valuable resources are being wasted" instead of "Valuable resources are being wasted by your company" or, even worse, "You are wasting valuable resources."

☐ Avoid taking responsibility for negative statements by attributing them to faceless, impersonal "others":
Say "It is more than possible that several objections to your proposed plans might be raised by some observers" or "Several objections might be raised by

those hostile to your plans" instead of "I have several objections to your plans."

☐ Use weasel words, especially if the reader is in a high-power position and will not like what you are saying.

☐ Use long sentences and heavy paragraphs to slow down the reader's comprehension of sensitive or negative information.

For a personal style

This style is usually appropriate in good-news and persuasive action-request situations.

☐ Use the active voice, which puts you, as the writer, at the front of sentences:
"Thank you very much for your comments" or "I appreciated your comments" instead of "Your comments were very much appreciated by me" or the even more impersonal "Your comments were very much appreciated."

☐ Use persons' names (first names, when appropriate) instead of referring to them by title:
"Bill James attended the meeting" instead of "Acme's director attended the meeting."

☐ Use personal pronouns—especially "you" and "I"—when you are saying positive things:
"I so much appreciate the work you've done" as opposed to "The work you've done is appreciated."

☐ Use short sentences that capture the rhythm of ordinary conversation:
"I discussed your proposal with Frank. He's all for it!" as opposed to "This is to inform you that your proposal was taken up at Friday's meeting and that it was regarded with favor."

☐ Use contractions ("can't," "won't," "shouldn't") to sound informal and conversational.

☐ Direct questions to the reader:
"Just ask yourself, how would your company like to save $10,000?"

☐ Interject positive personal thoughts and references that will make the reader know that this letter is really to him or her and not some type of form letter sent to just anyone.

For an impersonal style

This style is usually appropriate in negative and information-conveying situations. It's always appropriate in technical and scientific writing and usually when you are writing to technical readers.

☐ Avoid using persons' names, especially first names. Refer to people, if at all, by title or job description:
"I would like to know what you think of this plan" instead of "What do you think of this, Herb?"
"Our vice president of finance" or "the finance department," not "Ms. Jones."

☐ Avoid using personal pronouns, especially "you" and "I" ("we" may be all right because the corporate we is faceless and impersonal):
"The logistics are difficult, and the idea may not work" instead of "I think you have planned things so that the logistics are difficult and your idea may not work." "We wonder if the idea will work" rather than "I don't think the idea will work."

☐ Use the passive voice to make yourself conveniently disappear when desirable:
"An error in the calculations has been made" instead of "I think your calculations are wrong."

☐ Make some of your sentences complex and some paragraphs long; avoid the brisk, direct, simple-sentence style of conversation.

For a colorful style

Sometimes a lively style is appropriate in good-news situations. It is most commonly found in the highly persuasive writing of advertisements and sales letters.

☐ Insert some adjectives and adverbs: Instead of "This proposal will save corporate resources," write "This (hard-hitting) (productivity-building) (money-saving) proposal will (easily) (surely) (quickly) (immediately) save our (hard-earned) (increasingly scarce) (carefully guarded) corporate resources."

☐ If appropriate, use a metaphor (A is B) or a simile (A is like B) to make a point: "Truly this program is a *miracle* of logical design." "Our solution strikes at the very *root* of Acme's problems." "This program is like *magic* in its ability to...."

For a less colorful style

By avoiding adjectives, adverbs, metaphors, and figures of speech, you can make your style less colorful. Such a style is appropriate for ordinary business writing and also results from:

☐ Blending the impersonal style with the passive style.

☐ Employing words that remove any semblance of wit, liveliness, and vigor from the writing.

Please bear in mind that these six styles are not mutually exclusive. There is some overlap. A passive style is usually far more impersonal than personal and also not very colorful. A forceful style is likely to be more personal than impersonal, and a colorful style is likely to be fairly forceful. Nevertheless, these styles are distinct enough to justify talking about them. If we fail to make such distinctions, style becomes a catchall term that means nothing specific. Even if not precise, these distinctions enable us to talk about style and its elements and to learn to write appropriately for each situation.

Discuss needs first

What conclusions can we draw from this discussion? Simply that, whether you write your own letters or have to manage the writing of subordinates, to be an effective communicator, you must realize that:

1   Each style has an impact on the reader.

2   Style communicates to readers almost as much as the content of a message.

3   Style cannot be isolated from a situation.

4   Generalizing about which style is the best in all situations is impossible.

5   Style must be altered to suit the circumstances.

6   Style must be discussed sensibly in the work situation.

These conclusions will be of obvious help to managers who write their own letters. But what help will these conclusions be to managers who direct assistants in the writing of letters? In many instances, writing assignments go directly to subordinates for handling. Often, manager and assistant have no chance to discuss style strategy together. In such cases, rather than merely submitting a response for a signature, the subordinate would be wise to append a note: e.g., "This is a very sensitive situation, I think. Therefore, I deliberately drew back into a largely impersonal and passive style." At least, the boss will not jump to the conclusion that the assistant has written a letter of low impact by accident.

When they do route writing assignments to assistants, superiors could save much valuable time and prevent mutual distress if they told the subordinates what style seemed strategically wise in each situation. Playing guessing games also wastes money.

And if, as is often the case, neither superior nor subordinate has a clear sense of what style is best, the two can agree to draft a response in one style first, and if that doesn't sound right, to adjust the style appropriately.

Those who write their own letters can try drafting several responses to tough but important situations, each in a different style. It's wise to sleep on them and then decide which sounds best.

Whether you write for yourself or for someone else, it is extremely unlikely that in difficult situations a first draft will be signed by you or anyone else. Only the amateur expects writing perfection on the first try. By learning to control your style and to engineer the tone of your communications, you can make your writing effective. ▽

Such stuff as style is made on

To Frank A. Nichols, Secretary, Concord Free Trade Club

Hartford, March 1885
Dear Sir:

I am in receipt of your favor of the 24th inst., conveying the gratifying intelligence that I have been made an honorary member of the Free Trade Club of Concord, Massachusetts, and I desire to express to the Club, through you, my grateful sense of the high compliment thus paid me.

It does look as if Massachusetts were in a fair way to embarrass me with kindnesses this year. In the first place a Massachusetts Judge has just decided in open court that a Boston publisher may sell not only his own property in a free and unfettered way, but may also as freely sell property which does not belong to him but to me—property which he has not bought and which I have not sold. Under this ruling I am now advertising that judge's homestead for sale; and if I make as good a sum out of it as I expect I shall go on and sell the rest of his property.

In the next place, a committee of the public library of your town has condemned and excommunicated my last book [*Adventures of Huckleberry Finn*], and doubled its sale. This generous action of theirs must necessarily benefit me in one or two additional ways. For instance, it will deter other libraries from buying the book and you are doubtless aware that one book in a public library prevents the sale of a sure ten and a possible hundred of its mates. And secondly it will cause the purchasers of the book to read it, out of curiosity, instead of merely intending to do so after the usual way of the world and library committees; and then they will discover, to my great advantage and their own indignant disappointment, that there is nothing objectionable in the book, after all.

And finally, the Free Trade Club of Concord comes forward and adds to the splendid burden of obligations already conferred upon me by the Commonwealth of Massachusetts, an honorary membership which is more worth than all the rest since it endorses me as worthy to associate with certain gentlemen whom even the moral icebergs of the Concord library committee are bound to respect.

May the great Commonwealth of Massachusetts endure forever, is the heartfelt prayer of one who, long a recipient of her mere general good will, is proud to realize that he is at last become her pet….

Your obliged servant
S. L. Clemens

To the gas company

Hartford, February 1, 1891
Dear Sirs:

Some day you will move me almost to the verge of irritation by your chuckle-headed Goddamned fashion of shutting your Goddamned gas off without giving any notice to your Goddamned parishioners. Several times you have come within an ace of smothering half of this household in their beds and blowing up the other half by this idiotic, not to say criminal, custom of yours. And it has happened again to-day. Haven't you a telephone?

Ys
S L Clemens

Effective Interpersonal Communication

Barriers and Gateways to Communication

By Carl R. Rogers and F. J. Roethlisberger

COMMUNICATION among human beings has always been a problem. But it is only fairly recently that management and management advisers have become so concerned about it and the way it works or does not work in industry. Now, as the result of endless discussion, speculation, and plans of action, a whole cloud of catchwords and catch-thoughts has sprung up and surrounded it.

The Editors of the REVIEW therefore welcome the opportunity to present the following two descriptions of barriers and gateways to communication, in the thought that they may help to bring the problem down to earth and show what it means in terms of simple fundamentals. First Carl R. Rogers analyzes it from the standpoint of human behavior generally (Part I); then F. J. Roethlisberger illustrates it in an industrial context (Part II).

— The Editors

Part I

It may seem curious that a person like myself, whose whole professional effort is devoted to psychotherapy, should be interested in problems of communication. What relationship is there between obstacles to communication and providing therapeutic help to individuals with emotional maladjustments?

Actually the relationship is very close indeed. The whole task of psychotherapy is the task of dealing with a failure in communication. The emotionally maladjusted person, the "neurotic," is in difficulty, first, because communication within himself has broken down and, secondly, because as a result of this his communication with others has been damaged. To put it another way, in the "neurotic" individual parts of himself which have been termed unconscious, or repressed, or denied to awareness, become blocked off so that they no longer communicate themselves to the conscious or managing part of himself; as long as

this is true, there are distortions in the way he communicates himself to others, and so he suffers both within himself and in his interpersonal relations.

The task of psychotherapy is to help the person achieve, through a special relationship with a therapist, good communication within himself. Once this is achieved, he can communicate more freely and more effectively with others. We may say then that psychotherapy is good communication, within and between men. We may also turn that statement around and it will still be true. Good communication, free communication, within or between men, is always therapeutic.

It is, then, from a background of experience with communication in counseling and psychotherapy that I want to present two ideas: (1) I wish to state what I believe is one of the major factors in blocking or impeding communication, and then (2) I wish to present

EDITORS' NOTE: Mr. Rogers' and Mr. Roethlisberger's observations are based on their contributions to a panel discussion at the Centennial Conference on Communications,

Northwestern University, October 1951. A complete report of this conference may be secured by writing to the Publications Office, Northwestern University, Evanston, Illinois.

what in our experience has proved to be a very important way of improving or facilitating communication.

Barrier: The Tendency to Evaluate

I should like to propose, as a hypothesis for consideration, that the major barrier to mutual interpersonal communication is our very natural tendency to judge, to evaluate, to approve (or disapprove) the statement of the other person or the other group. Let me illustrate my meaning with some very simple examples. Suppose someone, commenting on this discussion, makes the statement, "I didn't like what that man said." What will you respond? Almost invariably your reply will be either approval or disapproval of the attitude expressed. Either you respond, "I didn't either; I thought it was terrible," or else you tend to reply, "Oh, I thought it was really good." In other words, your primary reaction is to evaluate it from *your* point of view, your own frame of reference.

Or take another example. Suppose I say with some feeling, "I think the Republicans are behaving in ways that show a lot of good sound sense these days." What is the response that arises in your mind? The overwhelming likelihood is that it will be evaluative. In other words, you will find yourself agreeing, or disagreeing, or making some judgment about me such as "He must be a conservative," or "He seems solid in his thinking." Or let us take an illustration from the international scene. Russia says vehemently, "The treaty with Japan is a war plot on the part of the United States." We rise as one person to say, "That's a lie!"

This last illustration brings in another element connected with my hypothesis. Although the tendency to make evaluations is common in almost all interchange of language, it is very much heightened in those situations where feelings and emotions are deeply involved. So the stronger our feelings, the more likely it is that there will be no mutual element in the communication. There will be just two ideas, two feelings, two judgments, missing each other in psychological space.

I am sure you recognize this from your own experience. When you have not been emotionally involved yourself and have listened to a heated discussion, you often go away thinking, "Well, they actually weren't talking about the same thing." And they were not. Each was making a judgment, an evaluation, from his own frame of reference. There was really nothing which could be called communication in any genuine sense. This tendency to react to any emotionally meaningful statement by forming an evaluation of it from our own point of view is, I repeat, the major barrier to interpersonal communication.

Gateway: Listening with Understanding

Is there any way of solving this problem, of avoiding this barrier? I feel that we are making exciting progress toward this goal, and I should like to present it as simply as I can. Real communication occurs, and this evaluative tendency is avoided, when we listen with understanding. What does that mean? It means to see the expressed idea and attitude from the other person's point of view, to sense how it feels to him, to achieve his frame of reference in regard to the thing he is talking about.

Stated so briefly, this may sound absurdly simple, but it is not. It is an approach which we have found extremely potent in the field of psychotherapy. It is the most effective agent we know for altering the basic personality structure of an individual and for improving his relationships and his communications with others. If I can listen to what he can tell me, if I can understand how it seems to him, if I can see its personal meaning for him, if I can sense the emotional flavor which it has for him, then I will be releasing potent forces of change in him.

Again, if I can really understand how he hates his father, or hates the company, or hates Communists — if I can catch the flavor of his fear of insanity, or his fear of atom bombs, or of Russia — it will be of the greatest help to him in altering those hatreds and fears and in establishing realistic and harmonious relationships with the very people and situations toward which he has felt hatred and fear. We know from our research that such empathic understanding — understanding *with* a person, not *about* him — is such an effective approach that it can bring about major changes in personality.

Some of you may be feeling that you listen well to people and yet you have never seen such results. The chances are great indeed that your listening has not been of the type I have described. Fortunately, I can suggest a little laboratory experiment which you can try to test the quality of your understanding. The next time you get into an argument with your wife, or your friend, or with a small group of friends, just stop the discussion for a moment and, for an experiment, institute this rule: "Each person can speak up for himself only *after* he has first restated the ideas and feelings of the previous speaker accurately and to that speaker's satisfaction."

You see what this would mean. It would simply mean that before presenting your own point of view, it would be necessary for you to achieve the other speaker's frame of reference — to understand his thoughts and feelings so well that you could summarize them for him. Sounds simple, doesn't it? But if you try it, you will discover that it is one of the most difficult things you have ever tried to do. However, once you have been able to see the other's point of view, your own comments will have to be drastically revised. You will also find the emotion going out of the discussion, the differences being reduced, and those differences which remain being of a rational and understandable sort.

Can you imagine what this kind of an approach would mean if it were projected into larger areas? What would happen to a labor-management dispute if it were conducted in such a way that labor, without necessarily agreeing, could accurately state management's point of view in a way that management could accept; and management, without approving labor's stand, could state labor's case in a way that labor agreed was accurate? It would mean that real communication was established, and one could practically guarantee that some reasonable solution would be reached.

If, then, this way of approach is an effective avenue to good communication and good relationships, as I am quite sure you will agree if you try the experiment I have mentioned, why is it not more widely tried and used? I will try to list the difficulties which keep it from being utilized.

Need for Courage. In the first place it takes courage, a quality which is not too widespread. I am indebted to Dr. S. I. Hayakawa, the semanticist, for pointing out that to carry on psychotherapy in this fashion is to take a very real risk, and that courage is required. If you really understand another person in this way, if you are willing to enter his private world and see the way life appears to him, without any attempt to make evaluative judgments, you run the risk of being changed yourself. You might see it his way; you might find yourself influenced in your attitudes or your personality.

This risk of being changed is one of the most frightening prospects many of us can face. If I enter, as fully as I am able, into the private world of a neurotic or psychotic individual, isn't there a risk that I might become lost in that world? Most of us are afraid to take that risk. Or if we were listening to a Russian Communist, or Senator Joe McCarthy, how many of us would dare to try to see the world from each of their points of view? The great majority of us could not *listen*; we would find ourselves compelled to *evaluate*, because listening would seem too dangerous. So the first requirement is courage, and we do not always have it.

Heightened Emotions. But there is a second obstacle. It is just when emotions are strongest that it is most difficult to achieve the frame of reference of the other person or group. Yet it is then that the attitude is most needed if communication is to be established. We have not found this to be an insuperable obstacle in our experience in psychotherapy. A third party, who is able to lay aside his own feelings and evaluations, can assist greatly by listening with understanding to each person or group and clarifying the views and attitudes each holds.

We have found this effective in small groups in which contradictory or antagonistic attitudes exist. When the parties to a dispute realize that they are being understood, that someone sees how the situation seems to them, the statements grow less exaggerated and less defensive, and it is no longer necessary to maintain the attitude, "I am 100% right and you are 100% wrong." The influence of such an understanding catalyst in the group permits the members to come closer and closer to the objective truth involved in the relationship. In this way mutual communication is established, and some type of agreement becomes much more possible.

So we may say that though heightened emotions make it much more difficult to understand *with* an opponent, our experience makes it clear that a neutral, understanding, catalyst type of leader or therapist can overcome this obstacle in a small group.

Size of Group. That last phrase, however, suggests another obstacle to utilizing the approach I have described. Thus far all our experience has been with small face-to-face groups — groups exhibiting industrial tensions, religious tensions, racial tensions, and therapy groups in which many personal tensions are present. In these small groups our experience, confirmed by a limited amount of research, shows that this basic approach leads to improved communication, to greater acceptance of others and by others, and to attitudes which are more positive and more problem-solving in nature. There is a decrease in defensiveness, in exaggerated statements, in evaluative and critical behavior.

But these findings are from small groups. What about trying to achieve understanding between larger groups that are geographically remote, or between face-to-face groups that are not speaking for themselves but simply as representatives of others, like the delegates at Kaesong? Frankly we do not know the answers to these questions. I believe the situation might be put this way: As social scientists we have a tentative test-tube solution of the problem of breakdown in communication. But to confirm the validity of this test-tube solution and to adapt it to the enormous problems of communication breakdown between classes, groups, and nations would involve additional funds, much more research, and creative thinking of a high order.

Yet with our present limited knowledge we can see some steps which might be taken even in large groups to increase the amount of listening *with* and decrease the amount of evaluation *about*. To be imaginative for a moment, let us suppose that a therapeutically oriented international group went to the Russian leaders and said, "We want to achieve a genuine understanding of your views and, even more important, of your attitudes and feelings toward the United States. We will summarize and resummarize these views and feelings if necessary, until you agree that our description represents the situation as it seems to you."

Then suppose they did the same thing with the leaders in our own country. If they then gave the widest possible distribution to these two views, with the feelings clearly described but not expressed in name-calling, might not the effect be very great? It would not guarantee the type of understanding I have been describing, but it would make it much more possible. We can understand the feelings of a person who hates us much more readily when his attitudes are accurately described to us by a neutral third party than we can when he is shaking his fist at us.

Faith in Social Sciences. But even to describe such a first step is to suggest another obstacle to this approach of understanding. Our civilization does not yet have enough faith in the social sciences to utilize their findings. The opposite is true of the physical sciences. During the war when a test-tube solution was found to the problem of synthetic rubber, millions of dollars and an army of talent were turned loose on the problem of using that finding. If synthetic rubber could be made in milligrams, it could and would be made in the thousands of tons. And it was. But in the social science realm, if a way is found of facilitating communication and mutual understanding in small groups, there is no guarantee that the finding will be utilized. It may be a generation or more before the money and the brains will be turned loose to exploit that finding.

Summary

In closing, I should like to summarize this small-scale solution to the problem of barriers in communication, and to point out certain of its characteristics.

I have said that our research and experience to date would make it appear that breakdowns in communication, and the evaluative tendency which is the major barrier to communication, can be avoided. The solution is provided by creating a situation in which each of the different parties comes to understand the other from the *other's* point of view. This has been achieved, in practice, even when feelings run high, by the influence of a person who is willing to understand each point of view empathically, and who thus acts as a catalyst to precipitate further understanding.

This procedure has important characteristics. It can be initiated by one party, without waiting for the other to be ready. It can even be initiated by a neutral third person, provided he can gain a minimum of cooperation from one of the parties.

This procedure can deal with the insincerities, the defensive exaggerations, the lies, the "false fronts" which characterize almost every failure in communication. These defensive distortions drop away with astonishing speed as people find that the only intent is to understand, not to judge.

This approach leads steadily and rapidly toward the discovery of the truth, toward a realistic appraisal of the objective barriers to communication. The dropping of some defensiveness by one party leads to further dropping of defensiveness by the other party, and truth is thus approached.

This procedure gradually achieves mutual communication. Mutual communication tends to be pointed toward solving a problem rather than toward attacking a person or group. It leads to a situation in which I see how the problem appears to you as well as to me, and you see how it appears to me as well as to you. Thus accurately and realistically defined, the problem is almost certain to yield to intelligent attack; or if it is in part insoluble, it will be comfortably accepted as such.

This then appears to be a test-tube solution to the breakdown of communication as it occurs in small groups. Can we take this small-scale answer, investigate it further, refine it, develop it, and apply it to the tragic and well-nigh fatal failures of communication which threaten the very existence of our modern world? It seems to me that this is a possibility and a challenge which we should explore.

Part II

In thinking about the many barriers to personal communication, particularly those that are due to differences of background, experience, and motivation, it seems to me extraordinary that any two persons can ever understand each other. Such reflections provoke the question of how communication is possible when people do not see and assume the same things and share the same values.

On this question there are two schools of thought. One school assumes that communication between A and B, for example, has failed when B does not accept what A has to say as being fact, true, or valid; and that the goal of communication is to get B to agree with A's opinions, ideas, facts, or information.

The position of the other school of thought is quite different. It assumes that communication has failed when B does not feel free to express his feelings to A because B fears they will not be accepted by A. Communication is facilitated when on the part of A or B or both there is a willingness to express and accept differences.

As these are quite divergent conceptions, let us explore them further with an example. Bill, an employee, is talking with his boss in the boss's office. The boss says, "I think, Bill, that this is the best way to do your job." Bill says, "Oh yeah!" According to the first school of thought, this reply would be a sign of poor communication. Bill does not understand the best way of doing his work. To improve com-

AUTHOR'S NOTE: For the concepts I use to present my material I am greatly indebted to some very interesting conversations I have had with my friend, Irving Lee. — *F. J. R.*

munication, therefore, it is up to the boss to explain to Bill why his way is the best.

From the point of view of the second school of thought, Bill's reply is a sign neither of good nor of bad communication. Bill's response is indeterminate. But the boss has an opportunity to find out what Bill means if he so desires. Let us assume that this is what he chooses to do, i.e., find out what Bill means. So this boss tries to get Bill to talk more about his job while he (the boss) listens.

For purposes of simplification, I shall call the boss representing the first school of thought "*Smith*" and the boss representing the second school of thought "*Jones.*" In the presence of the so-called same stimulus each behaves differently. Smith chooses to *explain*; Jones chooses to *listen*. In my experience Jones's response works better than Smith's. It works better because Jones is making a more proper evaluation of what is taking place between him and Bill than Smith is. Let us test this hypothesis by continuing with our example.

What Smith Assumes, Sees, and Feels

Smith assumes that he understands what Bill means when Bill says, "Oh yeah!" so there is no need to find out. Smith is sure that Bill does not understand why this is the best way to do his job, so Smith has to tell him. In this process let us assume Smith is logical, lucid, and clear. He presents his facts and evidence well. But, alas, Bill remains unconvinced. What does Smith do? Operating under the assumption that what is taking place between him and Bill is something essentially logical,

Smith can draw only one of two conclusions: either (1) he has not been clear enough, or (2) Bill is too damned stupid to understand. So he either has to "spell out" his case in words of fewer and fewer syllables or give up. Smith is reluctant to do the latter, so he continues to explain. What happens?

If Bill still does not accept Smith's explanation of why this is the best way for him to do his job, a pattern of interacting feelings is produced of which Smith is often unaware. The more Smith cannot get Bill to understand him, the more frustrated Smith becomes and the more Bill becomes a threat to his logical capacity. Since Smith sees himself as a fairly reasonable and logical chap, this is a difficult feeling to accept. It is much easier for him to perceive Bill as uncooperative or stupid. This perception, however, will affect what Smith says and does. Under these pressures Bill comes to be evaluated more and more in terms of Smith's values. By this process Smith tends to treat Bill's values as unimportant. He tends to deny Bill's uniqueness and difference. He treats Bill as if he had little capacity for self-direction.

Let us be clear. Smith does not see that he is doing these things. When he is feverishly scratching hieroglyphics on the back of an envelope, trying to explain to Bill why this is the best way to do his job, Smith is trying to be helpful. He is a man of goodwill, and he wants to set Bill straight. This is the way Smith sees himself and his behavior. But it is for this very reason that Bill's "Oh yeah!" is getting under Smith's skin.

"How dumb can a guy be?" is Smith's attitude, and unfortunately Bill will hear that more than Smith's good intentions. Bill will feel misunderstood. He will not see Smith as a man of goodwill trying to be helpful. Rather he will perceive him as a threat to his self-esteem and personal integrity. Against this threat Bill will feel the need to defend himself at all cost. Not being so logically articulate as Smith, Bill expresses this need, again, by saying, "Oh yeah!"

What Jones Assumes, Sees, and Feels

Let us leave this sad scene between Smith and Bill, which I fear is going to terminate by Bill's either leaving in a huff or being kicked out of Smith's office. Let us turn for a moment to Jones and see what he is assuming, seeing, hearing, feeling, doing, and saying when he interacts with Bill.

Jones, it will be remembered, does not assume that he knows what Bill means when he says, "Oh yeah!" so he has to find out. Moreover, he assumes that when Bill said this, he had not exhausted his vocabulary or his feelings. Bill may not necessarily mean one thing; he may mean several different things. So Jones decides to listen.

In this process Jones is not under any illusion that what will take place will be eventually logical. Rather he is assuming that what will take place will be primarily an interaction of feelings. Therefore, he cannot ignore the feelings of Bill, the effect of Bill's feelings on him, or the effect of his feelings on Bill. In other words, he cannot ignore his relationship to Bill; he cannot assume that it will make no difference to what Bill will hear or accept.

Therefore, Jones will be paying strict attention to all of the things Smith has ignored. He will be addressing himself to Bill's feelings, his own, and the interactions between them.

Jones will therefore realize that he has ruffled Bill's feelings with his comment, "I think, Bill, this is the best way to do your job." So instead of trying to get Bill to understand him, he decides to try to understand Bill. He does this by encouraging Bill to speak. Instead of telling Bill how he should feel or think, he asks Bill such questions as, "Is this what you feel?" "Is this what you see?" "Is this what you assume?" Instead of ignoring Bill's evaluations as irrelevant, not valid, inconsequential, or false, he tries to understand Bill's reality as he feels it, perceives it, and assumes it to be. As Bill begins to open up, Jones's curiosity is piqued by this process.

"Bill isn't so dumb; he's quite an interesting guy" becomes Jones's attitude. And that is what Bill hears. Therefore Bill feels understood and accepted as a person. He becomes less defensive. He is in a better frame of mind to explore and re-examine his own perceptions, feelings, and assumptions. In this process he perceives Jones as a source of help. Bill feels free to express his differences. He feels that Jones has some respect for his capacity for self-direction. These positive feelings toward Jones make Bill more inclined to say, "Well, Jones, I don't quite agree with you that this is the best way to do my job, but I'll tell you what I'll do. I'll try to do it that way for a few days, and then I'll tell you what I think."

Conclusion

I grant that my two orientations do not work themselves out in practice in quite so simple or neat a fashion as I have been able to work them out on paper. There are many other ways in which Bill could have responded to Smith in the first place. He might even have said, "O.K., boss, I agree that your way of doing my job is better." But Smith still would not have known how Bill felt when he made this statement or whether Bill was actually going to do his job differently. Likewise, Bill could have responded to Jones in a way different from my example. In spite of Jones's attitude, Bill might still be reluctant to express himself freely to his boss.

The purpose of my examples has not been to demonstrate the right or wrong way of communicating. My purpose has been simply to provide something concrete to point to when I make the following generalizations:

(1) Smith represents to me a very common pattern of misunderstanding. The misunderstanding does not arise because Smith is not clear enough in expressing himself. It arises because of Smith's misevaluation of what is taking place when two people are talking together.

(2) Smith's misevaluation of the process of personal communication consists of certain very common assumptions, e.g., (a) that what is taking place is something essentially logical; (b) that words in themselves apart from the people involved mean something; and (c) that the purpose of the interaction is to get Bill to see things from Smith's point of view.

(3) Because of these assumptions, a chain reaction of perceptions and negative feelings is engendered which blocks communication. By ignoring Bill's feelings and by rationalizing his own, Smith ignores his relationship to Bill as one of the most important determinants of the communication. As a result, Bill hears Smith's attitude more clearly than the logical content of Smith's words. Bill feels that his individual uniqueness is being denied. His personal integrity being at stake, he becomes defensive and belligerent. As a result, Smith feels frustrated. He perceives Bill as stupid. So he says and does things which only provoke more defensiveness on the part of Bill.

(4) In the case of Jones, I have tried to show what might possibly happen if we made a different evaluation of what is taking place when two people are talking together. Jones makes a different set of assumptions. He assumes (a) that what is taking place between him and Bill is an interaction of sentiments; (b) that Bill — not his words in themselves — means something; (c) that the object of the interaction is to give Bill an opportunity to express freely his differences.

(5) Because of these assumptions, a psychological chain reaction of reinforcing feelings and perceptions is set up which facilitates communication between Bill and him. When Jones addresses himself to Bill's feelings and perceptions from Bill's point of view, Bill feels understood and accepted as a person; he feels free to express his differences. Bill sees Jones as a source of help; Jones sees Bill as an interesting person. Bill in turn becomes more cooperative.

(6) If I have identified correctly these very common patterns of personal communication, then some interesting hypotheses can be stated:

(a) Jones's method works better than Smith's, not because of any magic, but because Jones has a better map than Smith of the process of personal communication.

(b) The practice of Jones's method, however, is not merely an intellectual exercise. It depends on Jones's capacity and willingness to see and accept points of view different from his own, and to practice this orientation in a face-to-face relationship. This practice involves an emotional as well as an intellectual achievement. It depends in part on Jones's awareness of himself, in part on the practice of a skill.

(c) Although our colleges and universities try to get students to appreciate intellectually points of view different from their own, very little is done to help them to implement this general intellectual appreciation in a simple face-to-face relationship — at the level of a skill. Most educational institutions train their students to be logical, lucid, and clear. Very little is done to help them to listen more skillfully. As a result, our educated world contains too many Smiths and too few Joneses.

(d) The biggest block to personal communication is man's inability to listen intelligently, understandingly, and skillfully to another person. This deficiency in the modern world is widespread and appalling. In our universities as well as elsewhere, too little is being done about it.

(7) In conclusion, let me apologize for acting toward you the way Smith did. But who am I to violate a long-standing academic tradition!

The busy executive spends 80% of his time . . .

LISTENING to PEOPLE

. . . and still doesn't hear half of what is said.

By Ralph G. Nichols
and Leonard A. Stevens

Recently the top executives of a major manufacturing plant in the Chicago area were asked to survey the role that listening plays in their work. Later, an executive seminar on listening was held. Here are three typical comments made by participants:

❡ "Frankly, I had never thought of listening as an important subject by itself. But now that I am aware of it, I think that perhaps 80% of my work depends on my listening to someone, or on someone else listening to me."

❡ "I've been thinking back about things that have gone wrong over the past couple of years, and I suddenly realized that many of the troubles have resulted from someone not hearing something, or getting it in a distorted way."

❡ "It's interesting to me that we have considered so many facets of communication in the company, but have inadvertently overlooked listening. I've about decided that it's the most important link in the company's communications, and it's obviously also the weakest one."

These comments reflect part of an awakening that is taking place in a number of management circles. Business is tied together by its systems of communication. This communication, businessmen are discovering, depends more on the spoken word than it does on the written word; and the effectiveness of the spoken word hinges not so much on how people talk as on how they listen.

The Unused Potential

It can be stated, with practically no qualification, that people in general do not know how to listen. They have ears that hear very well, but seldom have they acquired the necessary aural skills which would allow those ears to be used effectively for what is called *listening*.

For several years we have been testing the ability of people to understand and remember what they hear. At the University of Minnesota we examined the listening ability of several thousand students and of hundreds of business and professional people. In each case the person tested listened to short talks by faculty members and was examined for his grasp of the content.

These extensive tests led us to this general conclusion: immediately after the average person has listened to someone talk, he remembers only about half of what he has heard — no matter how carefully he thought he was listening.

What happens as time passes? Our own testing shows — and it has been substantiated by reports of research at Florida State University and Michigan State University [1] — that two months after listening to a talk, the average

AUTHORS' NOTE: The material for this article comes from our forthcoming book, *Are You Listening?* (New York, McGraw-Hill Book Company, Inc., scheduled for publication September, 1957).

[1] See E. J. J. Kramar and Thomas R. Lewis, "Comparison of Visual and Nonvisual Listening," *Journal of Communication*, November 1951, p. 16; and Arthur W. Heilman, "An Investigation in Measuring and Improving Listening Ability of College Freshmen," *Speech Monographs*, November 1951, p. 308.

listener will remember only about 25% of what was said. In fact, after we have barely learned something, we tend to forget from one-half to one-third of it *within eight hours*; it is startling to realize that frequently we forget more in this first short interval than we do in the next six months.

Gap in Training

Behind this widespread inability to listen lies, in our opinion, a major oversight in our system of classroom instruction. We have focused attention on reading, considering it the primary medium by which we learn, and we have practically forgotten the art of listening. About six years are devoted to formal reading instruction in our school systems. Little emphasis is placed on speaking, and almost no attention has been given to the skill of listening, strange as this may be in view of the fact that so much lecturing is done in college. Listening training — if it could be called training — has often consisted merely of a series of admonitions extending from the first grade through college: "Pay attention!" "Now get this!" "Open your ears!" "Listen!"

Certainly our teachers feel the need for good listening. Why then have so many years passed without educators developing formal methods of teaching students to listen? We have been faced with several false assumptions which have blocked the teaching of listening. For example:

(1) We have assumed that listening ability depends largely on intelligence, that "bright" people listen well, and "dull" ones poorly. There is no denying that low intelligence has something to do with inability to listen, but we have greatly exaggerated its importance. A poor listener is not necessarily an unintelligent person. To be good listeners we must apply certain skills that are acquired through either experience or training. If a person has not acquired these listening skills, his ability to understand and retain what he hears will be low. This can happen to people with both high and low levels of intelligence.

(2) We have assumed that learning to read will automatically teach one to listen. While some of the skills attained through reading apply to listening, the assumption is far from completely valid. Listening is a different activity from reading and requires different skills. Research has shown that reading and listening skills do not improve at the same rate when only reading is taught.

This means that in our schools, where little attention is paid to the aural element of communica-

tion, reading ability is continually upgraded while listening ability, left to falter along on its own, actually degenerates. As a fair reader and a bad listener, the typical student is graduated into a society where the chances are high that he will have to listen about three times as much as he reads.

The barriers to listening training that have been built up by such false assumptions are coming down. Educators are realizing that listening is a skill that can be taught. In Nashville, for example, the public school system has started training in listening from elementary grades through high school. Listening is also taught in the Phoenix school system, in Cincinnati, and throughout the state of North Dakota. About two dozen major universities and colleges in the country now provide courses in listening.

At the University of Minnesota we have been presenting a course in listening to a large segment of the freshman class. Each group of students that has taken listening training has improved at least 25% in ability to understand the spoken word. Some of the groups have improved as much as 40%. We have also given a course in listening for adult education classes made up mostly of business and professional people. These people have made some of the highest gains in listening ability of any that we have seen. During one period, 60 men and women nearly doubled their listening test scores after working together on this skill one night a week for 17 weeks.

Ways to Improvement

Any course or any effort that will lead to listening improvement should do two things:

1. Build awareness to factors that affect listening ability.
2. Build the kind of aural experience that can produce good listening habits.

At least a start on the first of these two educational elements can be made by readers of this article; a certain degree of awareness is developed by merely discussing factors that affect listening ability. Later we shall discuss some steps that might be taken in order to work at the second element.

Tracks & Sidetracks

In general, people feel that concentration while listening is a greater problem than concentration during any other form of personal communication. Actually, listening concentration *is* more difficult. When we listen, concentration must be achieved despite a factor that is peculiar to aural communication, one of which few people are aware.

Basically, the problem is caused by the fact that we think much faster than we talk. The average rate of speech for most Americans is around 125 words per minute. This rate is slow going for the human brain, which is made up of more than 13 billion cells and operates in such a complicated but efficient manner that it makes the great, modern digital computers seem slow-witted. People who study the brain are not in complete agreement on how it functions when we think, but most psychologists believe that the basic medium of thought is language. Certainly words play a large part in our thinking processes, and the words race through our brains at speeds much higher than 125 words per minute. This means that, when we listen, we ask our brain to receive words at an extremely slow pace compared with its capabilities.

It might seem logical to slow down our thinking when we listen so as to coincide with the 125-word-per-minute speech rate, but slowing down thought processes seems to be a very difficult thing to do. When we listen, therefore, we continue thinking at high speed while the spoken words arrive at low speed. In the act of listening, the differential between thinking and speaking rates means that our brain works with hundreds of words in addition to those that we hear, assembling thoughts other than those spoken to us. To phrase it another way, we can listen and still have some spare time for thinking.

The use, or misuse, of this spare thinking time holds the answer to how well a person can concentrate on the spoken word.

Case of the Disenchanted Listener. In our studies at the University of Minnesota, we find most people do not use their spare thinking time wisely as they listen. Let us illustrate how this happens by describing a familiar experience:

A, the boss, is talking to B, the subordinate, about a new program that the firm is planning to launch. B is a poor listener. In this instance, he tries to listen well, but he has difficulty concentrating on what A has to say.

A starts talking and B launches into the listening process, grasping every word and phrase that comes into his ears. But right away B finds that, be-cause of A's slow rate of speech, he has time to think of things other than the spoken line of thought. Subconsciously, B decides to sandwich a few thoughts of his own into the aural ones that are arriving so slowly. So B quickly dashes out onto a mental sidetrack and thinks something like this: "Oh, yes, before I leave I want to tell A about the big success of the meeting I called yesterday." Then B comes back to A's spoken line of thought and listens for a few more words.

There is plenty of time for B to do just what he has done, dash away from what he hears and then return quickly, and he continues taking sidetracks to his own private thoughts. Indeed, he can hardly avoid doing this because over the years the process has become a strong aural habit of his.

But, sooner or later, on one of the mental sidetracks, B is almost sure to stay away too long. When he returns, A is moving along ahead of him. At this point it becomes harder for B to understand A, simply because B has missed part of the oral message. The private mental sidetracks become more inviting than ever, and B slides off onto several of them. Slowly he misses more and more of what A has to say.

When A is through talking, it is safe to say that B will have received and understood less than half of what was spoken to him.

Rules for Good Reception

A major task in helping people to listen better is teaching them to use their spare thinking time efficiently as they listen. What does "efficiently" mean? To answer this question, we made an extensive study of people's listening habits, especially trying to discover what happens when people listen well.

We found that good listeners regularly engage in four mental activities, each geared to the oral discourse and taking place concurrently with that oral discourse. All four of these mental activities are neatly coordinated when listening works at its best. They tend to direct a maximum amount of thought to the message being received, leaving a minimum amount of time for mental excursions on sidetracks leading away from the talker's thought. Here are the four processes:

(1) The listener thinks ahead of the talker, trying to anticipate what the oral discourse is leading to and what conclusions will be drawn from the words spoken at the moment.

(2) The listener weighs the evidence used by the talker to support the points that he makes. "Is this evidence valid?" the listener asks himself. "Is it the complete evidence?"

(3) Periodically the listener reviews and mentally summarizes the points of the talk completed thus far.

(4) Throughout the talk, the listener "listens between the lines" in search of meaning that is not necessarily put into spoken words. He pays attention to nonverbal communication (facial expressions, gestures, tone of voice) to see if it adds meaning to the spoken words. He asks himself, "Is the talker purposely skirting some area of the subject? Why is he doing so?"

The speed at which we think compared to that at which people talk allows plenty of time to accomplish these four mental tasks when we listen; however, they do require practice before they can become part of the mental agility that makes for good listening. In our training courses we have devised aural exercises designed to give people this practice and thereby build up good habits of aural concentration.

Listening for Ideas

Another factor that affects listening ability concerns the reconstruction of orally communicated thoughts once they have been received by the listener. To illustrate:

The newspapers reported not too long ago that a church was torn down in Europe and shipped stone by stone to America, where it was reassembled in its original form. The moving of the church is analogous to what happens when a person speaks and is understood by a listener. The talker has a thought. To transmit his thought, he takes it apart by putting it into words. The words, sent through the air to the listener, must then be mentally reassembled into the original thought if they are to be thoroughly understood. But most people do not know what to listen for, and so cannot reconstruct the thought.

For some reason many people take great pride in being able to say that above all they try to "get the facts" when they listen. It seems logical enough to do so. If a person gets all the facts, he should certainly understand what is said to him. Therefore, many people try to memorize every single fact that is spoken. With such practice at "getting the facts," the listener, we can safely assume, will develop a serious bad listening habit.

Memorizing facts is, to begin with, a virtual impossibility for most people in the listening situation. As one fact is being memorized, the whole, or part, of the next fact is almost certain to be missed. When he is doing his very best, the listener is likely to catch only a few facts, garble many others, and completely miss the remainder. Even in the case of people who *can* aurally assimilate all the facts that they hear, one at a time as they hear them, listening is still likely to be at a low level; they are concerned with the pieces of what they hear and tend to miss the broad areas of the spoken communication.

When people talk, they want listeners to understand their *ideas*. The facts are useful chiefly for constructing the ideas. Grasping ideas, we have found, is the skill on which the good listener concentrates. He remembers facts only long enough to understand the ideas that are built from them. But then, almost miraculously, grasping an idea will help the listener to remember the supporting facts more effectively than does the person who goes after facts alone. This listening skill is one which definitely can be taught, one in which people can build experience leading toward improved aural communication.

Emotional Filters

In different degrees and in many different ways, listening ability is affected by our emotions.[2] Figuratively we reach up and mentally turn off what we do not want to hear. Or, on the other hand, when someone says what we especially want to hear, we open our ears wide, accepting everything — truths, half-truths, or fiction. We might say, then, that our emotions act as aural filters. At times they in effect cause deafness, and at other times they make listening altogether too easy.

If we hear something that opposes our most deeply rooted prejudices, notions, convictions, mores, or complexes, our brains may become overstimulated, and not in a direction that leads to good listening. We mentally plan a rebuttal to what we hear, formulate a question designed to embarrass the talker, or perhaps simply turn to thoughts that support our own feelings on the subject at hand. For example:

The firm's accountant goes to the general manager and says: "I have just heard from the Bureau of Internal Revenue, and . . . ." The general manager suddenly breathes harder as he thinks, "That blasted bureau! Can't they leave me alone? Every year the government milks my profits to a point where . . . ." Red in the face, he whirls

[2] See Wendell Johnson, "The Fateful Process of Mr. A Talking to Mr. B," HBR January–February 1953, p. 49.

and stares out the window. The label "Bureau of Internal Revenue" cuts loose emotions that stop the general manager's listening.

In the meantime, the accountant may go on to say that here is a chance to save $3,000 this year if the general manager will take a few simple steps. The fuming general manager may hear this — if the accountant presses hard enough — but the chances are he will fail to comprehend it.

When emotions make listening too easy, it usually results from hearing something which supports the deeply rooted inner feelings that we hold. When we hear such support, our mental barriers are dropped and everything is welcomed. We ask few questions about what we hear; our critical faculties are put out of commission by our emotions. Thinking drops to a minimum because we are hearing thoughts that we have harbored for years in support of our inner feelings. It is good to hear someone else think those thoughts, so we lazily enjoy the whole experience.

What can we do about these emotional filters? The solution is not easy in practice, although it can be summed up in this simple admonition: *hear the man out.* Following are two pointers that often help in training people to do this:

(1) *Withhold evaluation* — This is one of the most important principles of learning, especially learning through the ear. It requires self-control, sometimes more than many of us can muster, but with persistent practice it can be turned into a valuable habit. While listening, the main object is to comprehend each point made by the talker. Judgments and decisions should be reserved until after the talker has finished. At that time, and only then, review his main ideas and assess them.

(2) *Hunt for negative evidence* — When we listen, it is human to go on a militant search for evidence which proves us right in what we believe. Seldom do we make a search for evidence to prove ourselves wrong. The latter type of effort is not easy, for behind its application must lie a generous spirit and real breadth of outlook. However, an important part of listening comprehension is found in the search for negative evidence in what we hear. If we make up our minds to seek out the ideas that might prove us wrong, as well as those that might prove us right, we are less in danger of missing what people have to say.

Benefits in Business

The improvement of listening, or simply an effort to make people aware of how important their listening ability is, can be of great value in today's business. When people in business fail to hear and understand each other, the results can be costly. Such things as numbers, dates, places, and names are especially easy to confuse, but the most straightforward agreements are often subjects of listening errors, too. When these mistakes are compounded, the resulting cost and inefficiency in business communication become serious. Building awareness of the importance of listening among employees can eliminate a large percentage of this type of aural error.

What are some of the specific problems which better listening can help solve?

Less Paper Work

For one thing, it leads to economy of communication. Incidents created by poor listening frequently give businessmen a real fear of oral communication. As a result, they insist that more and more communication should be put into writing. A great deal of communication needs to be on the record, but the pressure to write is often carried too far. The smallest detail becomes "memoed." Paper work piles higher and higher and causes part of the tangle we call red tape. Many times less writing and more speaking would be advisable — *if* we could plan on good listening.

Writing and reading are much slower communication elements than speaking and listening. They require more personnel, more equipment, and more space than do speaking and listening. Often a stenographer and a messenger are needed, to say nothing of dictating machines, typewriters, and other writing materials. Few people ever feel it is safe to throw away a written communication; so filing equipment is needed, along with someone to do the filing.

In oral communication there are more human senses at work than in the visual; and if there is good listening, more can often be communicated in one message. And, perhaps most important of all, there is the give-and-take feature of oral communication. If the listener does not understand a message, he has the opportunity to straighten matters out then and there.

Upward Communication

The skill of listening becomes extremely important when we talk about "upward communication." There are many avenues through which management can send messages downward through a business organization, but there are few avenues for movement of information in the upward direction. Perhaps the most obvious of the upward avenues is the human chain of people talking to people: the man working at the bench talks to his foreman, the foreman to his superintendent, the superintendent to his boss; and, relayed from person to person, the information eventually reaches the top.

This communication chain has potential, but it seldom works well because it is full of bad listeners. There can be failure for at least three reasons:

- Without good listeners, people do not talk freely and the flow of communication is seldom set in motion.
- If the flow should start, only one bad listener is needed to stop its movement toward the top.
- Even if the flow should continue to the top, the messages are likely to be badly distorted along the way.

It would be absurd to assume that these upward communication lines could be made to operate without hitches, but there is no reason to think that they cannot be improved by better listening. But the first steps must be taken by top management people. More and better listening on their part can prime the pumps that start the upward flow of information.

Human Relations

People in all phases of business need to feel free to talk to their superiors and to know they will be met with sympathetic understanding. But too many superiors — although they announce that their doors are always open — fail to listen; and their subordinates, in the face of this failure, do not feel free to say what they want to say. As a result, subordinates withdraw from their superiors more and more. They fail to talk about important problems that should be aired for both parties' benefit. When such problems remain unaired, they often turn into unrealistic monsters that come back to plague the superior who failed to listen.

The remedy for this sort of aural failure — and it should be applied when subordinates feel the need to talk — is what we have called "nondirective listening." The listener hears, really tries to understand, and later shows understanding by taking action if it is required. Above all, during an oral discourse, the listener refrains from firing his own thoughts back at the person

talking or from indicating his displeasure or disapproval by his mannerisms or gestures; he speaks up only to ask for clarification of a point.

Since the listener stands the chance of hearing that his most dearly held notions and ideas may be wrong, this is not an easy thing to do. To listen nondirectively without fighting back requires more courage than most of us can muster. But when nondirective listening can be applied, the results are usually worth the effort. The persons talking have a chance to unburden themselves. Equally important, the odds are better that the listener can counsel or act effectively when the time comes to make a move.

Listening is only one phase of human relations, only one aspect of the administrator's job; by itself it will solve no major problems. Yet the past experience of many executives and organizations leaves no doubt, in our opinion, that better listening can lead to a reduction of the human frictions which beset many businesses today.

Listening to Sell

High-pressure salesmanship is rapidly giving way to low-pressure methods in the marketing of industrial and consumer goods. Today's successful salesman is likely to center his attention on the customer-problem approach of selling.

To put this approach to work, the skill of listening becomes an essential tool for the salesman, while his vocal agility becomes less important. *How* a salesman talks turns out to be relatively unimportant because *what* he says, when it is guided by his listening, gives power to the spoken word. In other words, the salesman's listening becomes an on-the-spot form of customer research that can immediately be put to work in formulating any sales talk.

Regardless of the values that listening may hold for people who live by selling, a great many sales organizations seem to hold to the conviction that glibness has magic. Their efforts at improvement are aimed mainly at the talking side of salesmanship. It is our conviction, however, that with the typical salesman the ability to talk will almost take care of itself, but the ability to listen is something in real need of improvement.

In Conference

The most important affairs in business are conducted around conference tables. A great deal has been said and written about how to talk at a conference, how to compromise, how to get problem-centered, and how to cope with certain types of individuals. All these things can be very important, but too frequently the experts forget to say, "First and foremost you must learn to listen at a conference."

The reason for this is simple when we think of the basic purpose for holding almost any conference. People get together to contribute their different viewpoints, knowledge, and experience to members of the group, which then seeks the best of all the conferees' thinking to solve a common problem. If there is far more talking than listening at a conference, however, the oral contributions made to the group are hardly worth the breath required to produce them.

More and better listening at any conference is certain to facilitate the exchange of ideas so important to the success of a meeting. It also offers many other advantages; for example, when participants do a good job of listening, their conference is more likely to remain centered on the problem at hand and less likely to go off on irrelevant tangents.

The first steps toward improved conference listening can be taken by the group leader. If he will simply make an opening statement calling attention to the importance of listening, he is very likely to increase the participants' aural response. And if the leader himself does a good job of listening, he stands the chance of being imitated by the others in his group.

Conclusion

Some businessmen may want to take steps to develop a listening improvement program in their companies. Here are 14 suggestions designed to carry on what we hope this article has already started to do — build awareness of listening.

(1) Devote an executive seminar, or seminars, to a discussion of the roles and functions of listening as a business tool.

(2) Use the filmed cases now becoming available for management training programs.[3] Since these cases present the problem as it would appear in reality, viewers are forced to practice good listening habits in order to be sure of what is going on — and this includes not only hearing the sound track but also watching the facial mannerisms, gestures, and motions of the actors.

(3) If possible, bring in qualified speakers and ask them to discuss listening with special reference to how it might apply to business. Such speakers are available at a number of universities where listening is being taught as a part of communication training.

(4) Conduct a self-inventory by the employees regarding their listening on the job. Provide everyone with a simple form divided into spaces for each hour of the day. Each space should be further divided to allow the user to keep track of the amount of time spent in reading, writing, speaking, and listening. Discuss the results of these forms after the communication times have been totaled. What percentage of the time do people spend listening? What might improved listening mean in terms of job effectiveness?

(5) Give a test in listening ability to people and show them the scores that they make. There is at least one standardized test for this purpose.[4] Discuss the meaning of the scores with the individuals tested.

(6) Build up a library of spoken-word records of literature, speeches, and so forth (many can be purchased through record stores), and make them available in a room that has a record player. Also, lend the records to employees who might wish to take them home to enjoy them at their leisure. For such a library, material pertinent to the employees' jobs might be recorded so that those who are interested can listen for educational purposes.

(7) Record a number of actual briefing sessions that may be held by plant superintendents or others. When new people go to work for the company, ask them to listen to these sessions as part of their initial training. Check their comprehension of what they hear by means of brief objective tests. Emphasize that this is being done because listening is important on the new jobs.

(8) Set up role-playing situations wherein executives are asked to cope with complaints comparable to those that they might hear from subordinates. Ask observers to comment on how well an executive seems to listen. Do his remarks reflect a good job of listening? Does he keep himself from becoming emotionally involved in what the subordinate says? Does the executive listen in a way which would encourage the subordinate to talk freely?

(9) Ask salesmen to divide a notebook into sections, one for each customer. After making a call, a salesman should write down all useful information received aurally from the customer. As

[3] See George W. Gibson, "The Filmed Case in Management Training," HBR May–June 1957, p. 123.

[4] Brown-Carlsen Listening Comprehension Test (Yonkers-on-Hudson, World Book Company).

the information grows, he should refer to it before each return visit to a customer.

(10) Where a sales organization has a number of friendly customers, invite some of the more articulate ones to join salesmen in a group discussion of sales techniques. How do the customers feel about talking and listening on the part of salesmen? Try to get the customers to make listening critiques of salesmen they encounter.

(11) In a training session, plan and hold a conference on a selected problem and tape-record it. Afterwards, play back the recording. Discuss it in terms of listening. Do the oral contributions of different participants reflect good listening? If the conference should go off the track, try to analyze the causes in terms of listening.

(12) If there is time after a regularly scheduled conference, hold a listening critique. Ask each member to evaluate the listening attention that he received while talking and to report his analysis of his own listening performance.

(13) In important management meetings on controversial issues try Irving J. Lee's "Procedure for 'Coercing' Agreement." [5] Under the ground rules for this procedure, which Lee outlined in detail in his article, the chairman calls for a period during which proponents of a hotly debated view can state their position without interruption; the opposition is limited to (a) the asking of questions for clarification, (b) requests for information concerning the peculiar characteristics of the proposal being considered; and (c) requests for information as to whether it is possible to check the speaker's assumptions or predictions.

(14) Sponsor a series of lectures for employees, their families, and their friends. The lectures might be on any number of interesting topics that have educational value as well as entertainment features. Point out that these lectures are available as part of a listening improvement program.

Not all of these suggestions are applicable to every situation, of course. Each firm will have to adapt them to its own particular needs. The most important thing, however, may not be what happens when a specific suggestion is followed, but rather simply what happens when people become aware of the problem of listening and of what improved aural skills can do for their jobs and their businesses.

[5] HBR January–February 1954, p. 39.

PEOPLE seem to be far more powerfully driven to talk at each other than to listen to each other, and when they do listen the kind of feedback they give the speaker — and the kind of reaction the speaker makes, in turn, to this feedback — appears distressingly often to be self-defensive and generally competitive, or insincere and thus misleading, rather than clarifying, honest, and co-operative.

To be highlighted in this connection is the strangely underestimated fact that listeners can and frequently do feel gravely threatened by speakers. . . .

What makes this problem so intriguing is that as a matter of objective fact nothing passes from speaker to listener except air waves and light waves and, as such, as manifestations of physical force, they are impressively weak! Viewed mechanically, the sheer physical effects they sometimes produce are not obviously credible. These really feeble waves commonly disturb the cardiovascular system, endocrine glands, autonomic nervous system, skeletal musculature, even the digestive system of the listener, with effects ranging all the way from increased heart rate and blanching of the skin to regurgitation and even loss of consciousness. . . . Meanwhile nothing except the gentlest of vibrations in the air and perfectly harmless reflections of light passes between speaker and listener — even when the speaker shouts, trembles, and jumps up and down violently. An effective awareness of this should go far to make listeners less fearful and speakers less confident of the threatening powers of words, particularly snarled or shouted words, as such.

Wendell Johnson, *Your Most Enchanted Listener*
New York, Harper & Brothers, 1956, pp. 184–186.

The hidden messages managers send

Managers can enhance their understanding of communication among people by attending to images, settings, and body language

Michael B. McCaskey

If a manager in an organization talks about making an "end run," what is he saying? Is he seeing life in the organization as a game; is he seeing it as hazardous and maybe nominating himself for a hero role; or is he merely saying he's going all the way with a project, regardless. The truth is we don't know what he's saying. It is all too easy both to interpret the metaphors others use to fit our own meanings and to ignore the fact that metaphors have idiosyncratic meanings that should be listened to. The author describes three ways managers convey messages about themselves and the ways they see the world. He encourages the reader to see these ways—their metaphors, office settings, and body language and tones that accompany their speech—as means of communicating. Just as speech or mathematics, these are languages that can be learned. With skill in them, a manager can see or hear what is really going on when people talk, what hidden messages we are sending all the time. The author gives some hints on what to look and listen for in trying to understand others, but he warns against simplistic interpretations: all messages occur in context.

Mr. McCaskey is associate professor of organizational behavior at the Harvard Business School. His current area of research involves how managers cope with ill-defined situations. He is finding that nonverbal communication and imagery are tools for dealing with ambiguity.

Photographs by Thomas Wedell.

In the course of an ordinary day, the typical general manager spends an extraordinary amount of time meeting and talking with people. Part and parcel of a manager's communication are the imagery, the place, and the body movements that he or she uses. Images, setting, and body language are not just adjuncts to communication. They carry the messages; and indeed, in some cases, they *are* the messages. As such they are tremendously important to a manager. Yet managers often pay only haphazard attention to them or, worse, presume that they are not gifted in these areas. The truth is we all use these ways of communicating—whether we are aware of them or not. The gift is in knowing *what* is being communicated.

Like mathematics, French, and accounting, these are languages that can be learned. With intelligent practice, for example, a person can learn to read and to speak "place"—that is, to understand the symbolic, territorial, and behavior-influencing aspects of physical settings. Imagery, place, and body language rarely provide definitive information; but they do provide a manager with a way of knowing that is not available through other message channels. With skill in these languages, a manager can develop instincts and a good "feel" for a problem that makes additional appreciation of its subtleties possible.

If managers pay close attention to these features embedded in their everyday work life, they will enhance their awareness of communicating with others. In this article, I will present some ideas for understanding and practicing the languages and will

Author's note: I would like to thank Luise Cahill Dittrich for her help on an earlier version of this article that appeared in Anthony G. Athos and John J. Gabarro, *Interpersonal Behavior: Communication and Understanding in Relationships* (Englewood Cliffs, N.J.: Prentice-Hall, 1978).

indicate the right direction the reader can take to learn more on his or her own.

Managers' words & their images

A senior vice president in a large New York bank is talking about the group he formerly worked with: "You hit the bird cage and everyone is on a new perch. People are always moving there. People move so fast, and they—whew! I got out of there before it all came down."

The imagery is very graphic and tells a lot about this man and the world he lives in. If you could listen to him a little more, you would not be surprised to learn that he does not have a traditional banking background. He sees himself as an entrepreneur and feels that, while most of them are attractively dressed and schooled, the other executives in the bank don't have any fire in their guts. En masse (he doesn't see them as individuals) "they" are "birds," which suggests he thinks they are pretty, caged, and—quite likely—fragile. One can sense the relief this man felt when he moved to a part of the bank where he could be active, be himself, be entrepreneurial.

When you pay close attention to the words other people use, you notice that most people draw characteristic verbal pictures of themselves and the world around them. The imagery and metaphors that a person most frequently uses can be clues to understanding the world he or she inhabits. These vivid kernels of speech are drawn from the sports world, from literature, from religion, and from other fields of personal interest or background. The imagery shows what's valued, what's feared, and what the speaker's behavioral rules are.

Consider the following examples of imagery:

> "It's like a fugue, everyone has a different part to play."

> "What we do here is drop back five and punt."

> "I am prepared to wait until hell freezes over."

> "One more snide comment, and I would have exploded."

A recurring use of metaphors might suggest that a person sees life in the organization as a game or is fatalistic about outcomes. Metaphors can also reflect an optimistic, a pessimistic, or even a confused outlook. Think of your own metaphors. Can they be characterized as earthy, poetic, or violent? Taken in context, words in metaphor can be clues to how another is feeling, to what he or she views as important.

Another major point about the verbal environment of managers is that words are symbols, the meanings of which can vary greatly depending on who is using them. This point is troublesome, because it seems so obvious and at the same time contradicts an assumption we usually make in our everyday behavior. I have talked with managers who assume that words are entities and that communicating with another is essentially a process of logically ordering those entities. They direct all their efforts toward getting the words right and presenting a logically structured train of thought in order to persuade.

Much of the communication between two people, however, implicitly involves sentiments and feelings. These feelings are attached to the different experiences that words connote for an individual. A typical conversation bumps along without either party paying close attention to the different experiences and, therefore, the different meanings that lie behind the words. We tend to assume that we are all referring to the same thing when we say "the boss," "a good report," "a viable alternative," and "a workable solution," but most likely we are not.

As you examine misunderstandings between two managers, you will often find that what fouls the channels of communication is their mutual assumption that they are using the same words to mean the same things. A division vice president and general manager of a large consumer products company was in the early stages of trying to inculcate a team management style for his top group of managers. At one meeting his marketing vice president asked, "Who is driving the bus?"—implying that no one was. This was a clear metaphor based on familiar experience, probably made stronger by the active connotation of "driving" and the echo of "bus" in the word *business*. However, the seemingly clear question sparked off heated disagreement. The senior executive heard the marketing vice president saying he was uncomfortable that there would not be one person in charge. That was not at all what the division vice president had meant to convey by team management.

What makes communication problematic is that people fail to recognize the personally distinctive ways in which others use words. As Fritz Roethlisberger puts it, "As a result, we fail to notice the differences, and we read into our experiences similarities where differences exist."[1]

Keeping the differences in mind, try listening to conversations somewhat differently from usual. You might hear the following three features of the verbal environment:

☐ Does the person use concrete or abstract words? Different people are comfortable with different levels of abstraction. Some people use vivid, concrete expressions; others favor "-ism" and "-ion" words that describe states and conditions. A "concrete" listener might simply reject out of hand—and not bother listening to—someone who talks at a more abstract level, and vice versa.

☐ Does the person joke and kid a lot? Joking is one of the few ways some managers permit risky statements to be made. American managers especially allow each other greater leeway in delivering a hard truth if it is packaged as part of a joke.

☐ Does the person say "I" or "we" more often? With whom does the person identify? For what groups is he or she willing to say, "We need to...."? In addition, a speaker who uses the royal or editorial "we" to refer to an action that he or she has obviously performed alone (royalty and editors excepted) can sound pompous.

The emotional baggage that words carry shows up in other ways as well. In an aerospace company, two managers disagreed about the best way to approach top management for renewed funding of a promising research project. On the one hand, the group research director wanted to "provide a menu of options." He wanted not only to give some choices but also to specify the range without dramatically posing the stakes. By using the word *menu* he was saying, in effect, "After all, everybody has to eat something—the question is what."

On the other hand, the project manager wanted the company to "bite the bullet." He wanted to challenge top management to do it right (that is, to put big funding behind the project) or not to do it at all. Complete with overtones of the American Wild West and palpable dangers, his phrasing depicts a situation in which a big step—even though painful or risky—was necessary for the long-run health of the project. In this case, both managers are using words as emotional flags; their phrasing expresses very different sets of assumptions, values, and readings of company mission and philosophy.

Emotional flag waving can, however, be a real impediment to discussion. When a manager assigns a pejorative word (such as a 'Casanova," "brown

nose," "Commie") to another's point of view, he is labeling that person. In labeling, a person is using a word to stop or impede thinking; it represents a quick put-down. Without making an effort to understand the other's meanings, a person using a label often cuts off any thoughtful response. If the label is couched in a witty jibe, the offended party may find it particularly difficult to continue the discussion in terms of the issues. A manager who is a third party to such an exchange can play a valuable role in identifying the labeling for what it is and in restating the matter for continued discussion.

Another important aspect of the verbal environment of managers is questions. Why are they so important? Questions often contain assumptions that not only frame the problem in a certain way but also tend to force its resolution to conform to the implicit assumption.

In the example used earlier, one executive asked, "Who is driving the bus?" As I indicated, the question as phrased contains the assumption that *one* person should be doing the driving. But it also contains the assumption that anyone else is a back-seat driver, which is bad enough in a passenger car, but frightening in a busload of back-seat drivers. Both assumptions are antithetical to a team management concept. From the division vice president's point of view, that was the wrong question to be asking, and he was savvy enough to make the assumption in the question explicit and to challenge it.

But aren't there other aspects of questions that a manager needs to attend to? Well, yes. Questions are not always what they appear to be. Some, like the one I just posed, are really disguised statements. Gestalt psychologist Fritz Perls would sometimes refuse to answer questions that patients put to him. He thought of them as traps, inviting him to be the power figure. He wanted people to acknowledge their own power and to face up to the statements they needed to make without hiding behind them as questions. In addition, Roethlisberger has noted that some (perhaps many) questions are so silly they don't deserve to be answered.[2]

Yet in the United States, people feel obliged to answer a question, even though answering should depend on whether the question is a good one, whether it is posed at the right time, and whether a person wants to answer. You might find it revealing to pay attention to the questions you and others ask in conversations. See how many of the questions are really statements. A question is *not* as simple as it seems.

Finally, in considering how people reveal themselves through the words they use, look out for

1. Fritz J. Roethlisberger, *Management and Morale* (Cambridge, Mass.: Harvard University Press, 1941), p. 98.

2. Roethlisberger, *Management and Morale*, p. 100.

"either/or" thinking. Some people habitually frame discussions in these terms: something is either right or wrong; you are either with me or against me; a job is either good or bad.

Studies of the development of the mind have found that either/or thinking characterizes the early stages of a young adult's development. In time, most people discover that life is multidimensional and does not fit into two neat categories. Under stress, however, one can return to dichotomized thinking; it becomes time to "throw the crooks out" without investigating either whether they really are crooks or whether throwing crooks out is the most appropriate response. It is much easier to stereotype the opposition—and let thinking and efforts to understand end there—than it is to search for a more complex truth.

When you hear yourself or another manager discuss a situation in either/or terms, you might examine whether a two-value framework is, in that situation, posing false choices. There may be ways to synthetically create a new solution that incorporates something of both sides. The discussion then moves from thinking in either/or terms to thinking in both/and terms.

Words and imagery provide clues to the meanings and the important values, assumptions, and experiences that lie behind a person's choice of words. Next I examine how the place and character of a physical setting can influence communication between two people.

The office & place of business

Depending on who they are and what kind of interactions they want with others, people use physical spaces in distinctive ways. Yet it often happens that both the receiver and the sender of messages about place are unaware of what is being communicated. A manager who becomes a little more thoughtful can better read what people are saying through their use of place. Managers can also examine their own physical settings to see if their arrangements influence behavior in ways that serve their ends.

The first thing to understand about place is that it represents territory. Animals mark off the range of their territory and defend it against intruders, and so does the human animal. Fences, doors, and boundary markers of all sorts separate what belongs

The reader might look at the accompanying photographs of office spaces and try to read what the occupants are saying about themselves and about the kinds of interactions with others that they are inviting.

The Editors

to one person from what belongs to the rest of the world. Boundaries give security and privacy, protecting one from unwanted encroachments by others (at least boundaries make the statement that they are unwanted). For example, after a heavy snowfall in some Boston neighborhoods, people will claim as theirs the part of the street they have shovelled for parking. While the car is away, they will mark their claims with chairs or trash cans and strenuously object should anyone try to move in on "their spot."

For people to have a sense of "their own" and "home" seems quite important. Basketball teams like UCLA and Notre Dame are especially tough to beat when they have the home-court advantage. Home is familiar, predictable, and mine. The importance of having one's own territory shows up in a study of communal space in Coventry, England. Contrary to what one might expect, those families that had their own yards fraternized more than the families who shared a communal yard.

In analyzing this finding, one commentator suggests, "In suburbs and small towns, people are more likely to talk across their backyards if the property line is indicated by a fence. Because this boundary helps them maintain territoriality, it actually brings neighbors closer together." [3] This observation echoes Robert Frost's famous line, "Good fences make good neighbors."

The importance of place as territory shows up in the office as well. When a boss and a subordinate meet, whose office do they use? If the boss is sensitive to place as territory, the purpose of the meeting will decide the question. To conduct an adversary discussion, to emphasize hierarchy and authority, or to give directions, the boss should hold the meeting in his or her office. If, however, the boss wants to reach out to the subordinate—to have a conversation more on the other's terms—he or she might well consider traveling to the subordinate's office.

I know a manager who took the territoriality of office to heart. Just before beginning a tough negotiation session at another manager's office, he managed to sit in the other's big, ostentatious chair. He made light of his sitting in it by remarking on the feel of the chair as he swiveled from side to side. The second man was sufficiently discomfited by this unusual tactic that he lost the home-court advantage.

3. David Dempsey, "Man's Hidden Environment," *Playboy*, May 1972, p. 108.

At the same time that place defines territoriality, other features of the setting also influence behavior, including the amount and type of interaction among people. Thomas Allen at MIT has studied communication patterns in R&D offices. He finds that beyond a distance of 25 or 30 yards personal interaction drops off markedly.[4] This suggests that a manager should physically locate together people in the organization who have the greatest need to talk to each other. If you are starting up a new team, locate core members close together, even if this means sacrificing status space for some members. When younger managers understand the dynamics of propinquity, they may try to locate their offices next to the boss's.

A manager can use the spaces in his or her office to influence the character of interactions there. For instance, many managers set up their offices with two different areas. In one, the manager talks across a desk to a person seated at the other side. Such an arrangement emphasizes the manager's authority and position. A subordinate is likely to feel that here the boss exercises a home-court advantage. In a second area, chairs are grouped around a coffee table or are placed at right angles to each other. Because this arrangement signals a willingness to downplay hierarchical differences, it encourages freer exchange and perhaps more sociable encounters.

Managers in a large financial services company I know are perfect examples of how people display instinctive reactions to physical settings. They have a marked preference for using one of four conference rooms, which are all alike except for the tables. Three of the rooms have rectangular tables that can be moved into squares or U-shapes; the fourth and most popular room has a round table. For reasons having to do with the culture and norms of this organization, the managers much prefer to work with each other around the round table.

Physical settings can be used in other ways to control interactions among people. A buyer for an electronics company housed in a building that lacked an elevator deliberately located his office on the third floor. A salesperson coming to the reception desk on the first floor would invariably be told that the buyer "could see you immediately." The salesperson would then trek the 40 steps to the buyer's office and, while still out of breath and somewhat disoriented, be greeted by the buyer.[5] In this case, physical setting was designed to control the interaction, beginning it on terms that put the salesperson at a disadvantage.

The impact these arrangements have on people is consistent with what cultural anthropologists have observed concerning people's sense of personal space. Edward T. Hall has studied how people in different cultures vary in what constitutes a comfortable distance for talking. His research shows that while the English and Germans stand farther apart than Americans when talking, the Arabs and Japanese stand closer together. Hall also identifies four basic distances for interaction: intimate space (touching to 18 inches); personal space (18 inches to 4 feet); social space (4 feet to 12 feet); and public space (12 feet and beyond).[6]

With chairs at right angles people can more easily move into each other's personal space. When a desk is placed between two people, the interaction shifts from a personal space to a social space. The content and nature of communication between two people change markedly when they move from one spatial zone to another. As a result of furniture arrangement, then, people often do become more distant—in both senses of the term.

The physical setting also influences behavior because it symbolizes the status of the occupants. Managers sense this, and one sometimes sees terrific battles fought over physical space in organizations as members vie for the visible manifestation of a more subtle and elusive phenomenon—power and influence. John Dean noticed this in his first days at the White House:

"As Bud and I went past the offices of White House staff members, I noticed furniture and files being moved. The White House, far more than any other government office, was in a state of perpetual internal flux. Offices were constantly exchanged and altered. . . .

"Everyone jockeyed for a position close to the President's ear, and even an unseasoned observer could sense minute changes in status. Success and failure could be seen in the size, decor, and location of offices. Anyone who moved to a smaller office was on the way down. If a carpenter or wallpaper hanger was busy in someone's office, this was a sure sign he was on the rise. Every day, workmen crawled over the White House complex like ants. Movers busied themselves with the continuous shuffling of furniture from one office to another as people moved in, up, down, or out. We learned to read office changes as an index of the internal bureaucratic power struggles."

4. Thomas J. Allen, "Communication Networks in R&D Laboratories," R&D Management, Vol. 1, 1970, p. 14.

5. Luise Cahill Dittrich, "The Psychology of Place," ICCH 9-476-086, distributed by the Intercollegiate Case Clearing House, Soldiers Field, Boston, Mass. 02163.

6. Edward T. Hall, The Hidden Dimension (New York: Doubleday, 1966).

7. John W. Dean III, Blind Ambition (New York: Simon & Schuster, 1976), p. 29.

By White House standards Dean's first office was shabby. When he complained, he was told it was only temporary, that Haldeman hadn't decided where to put him yet: "I did not have to be told what was happening. I was being tested and my performance would determine what I would get. I was at the bottom of the ladder, and instinctively, I began to climb." [7]

From the manager's point of view control over personal furnishings enhances power and authority. Or, depending on how he uses his office, the manager can emphasize other values that he considers essential to the high performance of the company.

Ken Olsen and the other top managers at Digital Equipment Corporation have built one of the most successful minicomputer companies in the world. Their offices in an old mill are far from grand. Sometimes separated by plywood partitions, the offices are faithful to the simple, Spartan beginnings of the company. These arrangements send very clear messages to the managers and to visitors—hard work and what is functional are important at DEC. Some may disagree with the DEC managers' choices now that they are so successful, but, regardless, they reveal the range possible in using physical space to support and convey the essential values of the organization.

Although it's easier to see when visiting another organization, you might tour your own and look at the messages you send by your use of physical space. Try touring it as if it were another company. How much of the space (and information) is locked up? Are files, phones, and offices fastened shut? How carefully do differences in the size, location, and furnishings of offices mark status?

Look at the bulletin boards. If they are extremely neat and if notices must be initialed, employees will feel less free to scrawl their own notes or to put up cartoons. Is there a coffee urn or somewhere else that serves as a "watering hole," or are people isolated from one another by the office layout? An informed reading of place can reveal a lot about how tight a company is, how hierarchical, how rules conscious, whether individual expression is encouraged, and what the company values.

Most individuals set up their office spaces to encourage certain types of interaction and, consciously or not, to send messages about themselves. When I enter a person's place for the first time, I often look at how much he or she has personalized it with pictures of family, mentors, friends, or favorite places. How much does that person declare about himself? Who are the special people, what kinds of things does he enjoy having around?

When you first walk into an office or a home, notice the textures. If the person had a choice, did he use tactile fabrics, long-haired rugs, coverings that invite a vistor to run a hand over them? This person may be signaling a desire to "be in touch," to interact at a closer distance. Or are the surfaces clean, polished, and smooth? Does the owner seem to prefer orderliness, to keep interactions at more of a distance? You might look at your own spaces in the same way and try to read the messages that others might find there about you and your preferred styles of interacting.

Body language & paralinguistics

Like physical settings, body language and paralinguistics convey important messages that color, support, or contradict the words people use. They send nonverbal messages, although in the case of paralinguistics (which includes the tone of voice, pacing, and other extralinguistic features that surround talking), they can involve sounds.

A project director in a huge aerospace company called a meeting of higher management people who supported his research project. Consonant with the oft-expressed company policy of commercially exploiting advanced research work, he wanted them to fund development of a new product internally. Early in the meeting, as he began to outline the sizable costs involved, he sensed their disapproval from facial expressions and body postures. His intuition told him that if they were asked to make an explicit decision on the project, it would be negative. So he changed his line of argument and began stressing the possibilities for external rather than internal funding of the project. And he assiduously avoided asking for a funding decision at that time.

This type of nonverbal communication and adjustment occurs every day in business, but frequently it goes unnoticed. Messages that are key to a situation—but that participants feel cannot be publicly or verbally acknowledged—are sent through these channels. Because nonverbal messages are ambiguous and subtle, one can readily reinterpret or deny them. Paradoxically, such messages can be safer and truer precisely because they are not precise. In the aerospace company, both the project director and higher management had their own reasons for keeping the communication ambiguous.

Several books have appeared lately in the popular press that claim to remove the ambiguity from body language. They offer a single translation for many facial expressions and body postures. For example, arms crossed against the chest "means" that the listener has closed his mind to what the speaker is saying. This kind of simplistic interpretation is an unfortunate misuse of the scholarly research on nonverbal communication. No gesture has a single, unvarying meaning. The researchers have stressed that the meaning of any gesture depends on cultural norms, personal style, the physical setting, what has gone before, and what both parties anticipate for the future.

Even when the person and the context are fairly well known, one should be cautious in interpreting body language. Recently I was walking down a company hallway with a staff person of a large manufacturer. We passed and exchanged greetings with a man named Jim who was just coming from a meeting where he had learned of his new assignment. His face was sagging, and his walk and carriage lacked their usual briskness.

Later at lunch we spent several minutes comparing our readings of Jim's nonverbal behavior, searching for alternative explanations, and wondering what each possibility might suggest for the department's future. Interpretations like this should be made cautiously and tentatively. We might find out, for example, that Jim was suffering from the flu—and that was the main source of his nonverbal behavior.

Keeping in mind that nonverbal languages are useful (because they are ambiguous) and the need for interpreting meanings within context, let us see how a manager could learn to read nonverbal languages with greater understanding. For many, the face is the most obvious conveyor of feelings—so obvious, in fact, that we have the expression, "It was written all over his face." Some research indicates that facial expression, along with tone of voice, accounts for more than 90% of the communication between two people. The dictionary meaning of words, then, accounts for only about 10% of the communication.[8]

The best way to improve one's reading of facial expressions is to watch soundless videotape or film of people's faces as they talk. Watch for raising or knitting of the eyebrows, widening of the pupils, flaring or wrinkling of the nose, tightening of the lips, baring or clenching of the teeth. To take one example, dilating pupils tend to mean that the listener is interested in what you are saying; contracting pupils suggest he or she does not like what you are saying.

But reading a facial expression is a complex process because a face often shows a mixture of several feelings at once, matching the mixture of feelings that the person may be experiencing inside.

Eye-to-eye contact is one of the most direct and powerful ways people communicate nonverbally. In U.S. culture, the social rules suggest that in most situations eye contact for a short period is appropriate. Prolonged eye contact is usually taken to be either threatening or, in another context, a sign of romantic interest. Most managers are aware that they look directly at individual members of an audience to enhance the impact of their presentation. Some, however, are not aware of how important eye contact is when they are listening. A good listener must be physically active to show good attention.

Among whites in the United States, the general rule is that the *speaker* in a conversation should find a way to break eye contact and look away. The *listener* shows attention by spending relatively more time looking at the speaker. Because it makes it harder for the speaker to continue, communication difficulties arise if the listener looks away too often. Knowing the impact looking away has can help a manager signal how much longer he or she wishes the other to continue speaking.

For example, in situations where the boss wishes to hear out the subordinate, he or she should be careful to provide the encouragement of eye attention, head nodding, and occasional "uh huhs" as the other is speaking. Even without saying words, a manager is sending nonverbal messages about the depth of his or her understanding and the degree of empathy.

The unspoken norms about patterns of eye contact do differ among racial groups. For blacks or Chicanos looking away does not necessarily mean the same lack of attention that it might mean among white speakers. A young white businessman learned this lesson in his first year of managing a subsidiary in a predominantly Chicano community. He was reprimanding a clerk named Carlos for a repeated error in record keeping. As he tried to discuss the matter, Carlos kept averting his eyes. The manager

8. Albert Mehrabian, "Communication Without Words," *Psychology Today*, September 1968, p. 52.

9. Erving Goffman, *Frame Analysis: An Essay on the Organization of Experience* (New York: Harper & Row, 1974), p. 543.

10. W.S. Condon and W.D. Ogston, "A Segmentation of Behavior," *Journal of Psychiatric Research*, Vol. 5, 1967, p. 221; and Albert E. Scheflen, *How Behavior Means* (Garden City, N.Y.: Doubleday, 1974).

11. Ray L. Birdwhitsell, *Kinesics and Context* (Philadelphia: University of Pennsylvania Press, 1970).

12. Frederick Erickson, "Gatekeeping and the Melting Pot: Interaction in Counselling Encounters," *Harvard Educational Review*, Vol. 45, February 1975, p. 44.

became angry and said, "Look at me when I'm talking to you." The young stock boy tried to establish eye contact but could not maintain it for long.

To the manager, this signaled disrespect and possibly defiance. For the stock boy (following his own cultural norms), it would have been a sign of disrespect to maintain eye contact with a boss who was reprimanding him. It was only after Carlos became extremely discomfited that the manager realized that Carlos's behavior was not meant to communicate disrespect. Thus patterns of nonverbal communication are highly variable among different cultures and groups, and one should be cautious in generalizing too broadly. Assuming that everyone follows the same rules can lead to misinterpretations.

The paralinguistic features of speech offer another powerful means of tuning in to another's feelings. How is something said? Paralanguage includes tone and quality of voice, pitch, pacing of speech, and sounds such as sighs or grunts. Managers can treat paralanguage as the music of communication—to observe how a person's voice tightens or catches at difficult passages or rushes and soars at moments of high emotion. Surprisingly, one can often hear the voice of another better without accompanying visual information. Because verbal messages can be distracting (an overload) or contradictory to the music of paralanguage, we do not attend as closely as we might to this valuable data source in face-to-face meetings.

Managers should notice pauses and silences as well as the pacing of speech. Silences can have a whole range of meanings. At one extreme, people use them as a weapon or tactic to close a sale or to seek agreement—waiting until the other is discomfited enough to make some concession toward their positions. Used another way, a pause in the conversation can be a valuable gift that allows the other person time to consider carefully his or her thoughts and feelings. The nonverbal behavior a person uses during the silence can help convey whether he or she intends one or the other effect.

One special type of pause is the *filled pause*, in which the speaker uses a sound such as "uhhh" to fill the spaces between words. Sociologist Erving Goffman notes that filled pauses are used to "provide continuity, showing that the speaker is still in the business of completing a reply even though he cannot immediately muster up the right words to effect this." [9] A filled pause is a signal that preserves the speaker's right to talk since it says, in effect, "Don't interrupt. I'm still talking."

The hidden messages of body language and paralanguage do not have to be the same as the verbal ones; and, in fact, a one-to-one correspondence is unlikely. But in situations where full and open communication is the aim, the nonverbal messages should add to the verbal ones in ways that are reasonable and trustworthy. When a person is communicating well, the body language moves in concert with the words. Smaller movements such as dropping the head, the hands, or the eye's gaze mark a pause, emphasize a point, or express some doubt or irony in one's speech. To mark larger transitions in thought, the speaker will change his body position altogether.[10] Nonverbal behavior, then, serves as punctuation for the verbal messages being sent.

In moments of great rapport, a remarkable pattern of nonverbal communication can develop. Two people will mirror each other's movements—dropping a hand, shifting their body at *exactly* the same time.[11] This happens so quickly that without videotape or film replay one is unlikely to notice the mirroring. But managers can learn to watch for disruptions in this mirroring because they are dramatically obvious when they occur. In the midst of talking, when a person feels that the other has violated his expectations or values, he or she will often signal distress. If norms or status differences make it unwise to express disagreement or doubt verbally, then the message will be conveyed through nonverbal "stumbles."

Instead of smooth mirroring, there will be a burst of movement, almost as if both are losing balance. Arms and legs may be thrust out and the whole body posture changed in order to regain balance.[12] Stumbles signal the need to renegotiate what's being discussed. The renegotiation occurs very rapidly and subtly and often through nonverbal channels. Managers who are aware of stumbles and what they mean have an option open to them that unaware managers do not. They can decide whether a given situation could be more effectively dealt with by verbally discussing it.

As with other languages, a manager can increase skill in sending nonverbal messages through intelligent practice. One helpful approach is to isolate and study one channel at a time. Because more information comes through several channels than one person can handle in a face-to-face encounter, for purposes of learning a person should try to latch on to one set of details at a time. Isolating a channel allows one to appreciate more fully the complexity and richness of each channel.

For example, one way managers can increase their listening skills and sharpen their appreciation of body language is by replaying videotapes of their own and others' behavior or by watching television without the sound. Listening to audiotapes and hearing the music of paralanguage is also instructive.

The nonverbal channels often convey messages too sensitive for explicit verbal communication. Since the messages are subtle, ambiguous, and often tentative, they must be read with caution in order to realize their potential richness. These hidden messages reinforce or contradict what is proclaimed verbally and thus can aid an aware manager in making sense of a situation.

Reading the messages

One of the ways a manager can develop skill in all three languages is to work in a small group. It's often instructive for managers to try out proposed solutions to a managerial problem by playing roles while others watch. The observers will often be surprised at how quickly they can tell if one of the role players is feeling under attack or is trying to mislead the other. Even though a role player thinks he is hiding his discomfort or impatience, observers read the hidden messages quite clearly, although the role players themselves may not be aware of them.

Two lessons emerge. First, for those who are uncomfortable with the idea that they may be giving themselves away, it is very difficult to censor these messages. They "leak out" one way or another. Trying to censor them only increases the confusion of signals and diverts energy that could better be directed toward understanding what is going on. Second, body language, paralinguistics, and imagery are always part of an interaction. The messages are there to be read. With practice a manager can increase skill in reading and sending these messages, even to the point of being able to attend to them while in the middle of a specific situation.

In summary, none of these three languages alone gives a clear-cut message about the people using them. But cumulatively they can form the basis for impressions and hunches to be checked out through further inquiry. Our physical settings, like the clothes we wear, the words we utter, and the gestures we make, communicate to others about us and influence others with regard to us. Whether we are aware of it or not, our interactions with people will be affected by what they learn about us through our imagery, settings, and body language—and by what we learn about them through theirs.▽

Editors' note: We are grateful to Mintz, Levin, Cohn, Glovsky and Popeo (pp. 29, 30, 31); Data Resources, Inc. (p. 33); and Thorndike, Doran, Paine & Lewis, Inc. (p. 32) for allowing us to photograph the office spaces that appear in this article.

Effective
Communication
in Groups

*How to overcome
the limits of trust and the
fear of candor*

Nobody Trusts the Boss Completely— Now What?

by Fernando Bartolomé

Managers who can head off serious problems before they blow up in the company's face are two steps ahead of the game. Their employers avoid needless expense or outright disaster, and they themselves get the promotions they deserve for running their departments smoothly and nipping trouble neatly in the bud.

Subordinates are never eager to give the boss bad news.

In practice, of course, it's never this easy. Everyone knows that one trick to dealing with problems is to learn about them early. But what's the trick to learning about them early? How do effective managers find out that trouble is brewing? What are their warning systems?

All good managers have their own private information networks, and many develop a kind of sixth sense for the early signs of trouble. But by far the simplest and most common way to find out about problems is to be told, usually by a subordinate.

It is easy to get information when things are going well. People love to give the boss good news. But subordinates are never eager to tell their supervisors that the latest scheme isn't working, to assume ownership of a problem by giving it a name, to look like an informer, or to sound like Chicken Little. A subordinate's reluctance to be frank about problems is also related to risk. While it's fairly easy to tell the boss that the machines sent over by the purchasing department aren't working properly, it's much harder to admit responsibility for the malfunction, and harder still—and perhaps dangerous—to blame it on the boss. Yet it is terribly important to get subordinates to convey unpleasant messages. The sooner a problem is disclosed, diagnosed, and corrected, the better for the company.

Almost any organization would operate more effectively with completely open and forthright employees, but absolute frankness is too much to hope for (and probably too much to bear). Candor depends upon trust, and in hierarchical organizations, trust has strict natural limits.

The Limits of Trust and Candor

In a hierarchy, it is natural for people with less power to be extremely cautious about disclosing weaknesses, mistakes, and failings—especially when the more powerful party is also in a position to evaluate and punish. Trust flees authority, and, above all, trust flees a judge. Managers are inescapably positioned to judge subordinates. Good managers may be able to confine evaluation to formal occasions, to avoid all trace of judgmental style in other settings, even to communicate criticism in a positive, constructive way. But there is no way to escape completely a subordinate's inclination to see superiors as judges.

So one of the limits on candor is self-protection. For example, people often hide the failures of their own departments and hope they will correct themselves. In one typical case, the development group for a piece of special software fell terribly behind on its

Fernando Bartolomé is professor of management at Bentley College in Waltham, Massachusetts. He is also guest lecturer at the European Institute of Business Administration (INSEAD) in France and at the Oxford Centre for Management Studies in England. He consults frequently in Europe, the United States, and Latin America. This is his fifth article for HBR.

*"Don't you have any feeling for this car, Mr. Geller?
Don't you ever communicate with it?"*

Sometimes a subordinate may try to protect a client. In one case, a salesman withheld the information that one of his largest customers was in financial trouble. The customer went bankrupt, and the company lost $500,000.

We can only guess at the salesman's motives—eagerness to get his commission before the troubled company failed, fear of losing an old customer, reluctance to give official warning of a danger that might be exaggerated. The fact remains that he failed to communicate the problem, his boss saw no sign of danger, and the company lost half a million dollars.

Often the motive for silence is at least superficially praiseworthy: people keep quiet about a developing problem while trying to solve it. Most believe solving problems on their own is what they're paid to do, and in many cases, they're right. Subordinates are not paid to run to their bosses with every glitch and hiccup. As problems grow more serious, however, managers need to know about them.

schedule, but no one told the manager until the delivery date could no longer be met. Delivery was three months late, and the company had to absorb a financial penalty.

The lack of candor was not self-protective in the long run, of course, because the development group was ultimately held responsible for the delay. But human beings are often shortsighted. At one time or another, most of us have chosen an uncertain future calamity over today's immediate unpleasantness.

A variation on this theme is when subordinates protect their own subordinates in order to protect themselves, as in the following example:

□ I was vice president of finance for a large manufacturing company and supervised a staff of 27. One new hire was failing on an important assignment. Her supervisor—who had hired her—withheld this information from me until her failure could no longer be corrected without serious disruption. He didn't tell me because he knew I would make him face up to the problem and deal with it, which he knew he would find very difficult to do.

The difficulty here lies in the bewildering territory between minor snags and major disasters. Handled promptly and decisively, the problems in this gray area sometimes turn out to be insignificant, but self-confident supervisors, particularly inexperienced ones, are perhaps too eager to prove they can cope on their own. This case is typical:

□ I am head of medical research in a pharmaceutical company. My job is part of R&D and is on the critical path to marketing any new product. One of my managers saw that we weren't receiving data critical to the timely generation of a licensing package for worldwide registration of a new drug. He spent four months trying to get the data on his own, or proceed without it, and didn't inform me of the problem. We suffered an eight-month delay in applying for a license to sell. That represents 10% of the patent life of the product, which has estimated peak worldwide sales of $120 million a year.

Politics is another common obstacle to candor. Organizations are political systems, and employees are often involved in political struggles. There is no guarantee your subordinates will be on your side.

A U.S. engineering-products company manufactured a successful product on license from a Swedish company, but the American CEO heartily disliked his Swedish counterpart and came to the private conclusion that the licensing fees were out of line. Knowing that his senior staff would object, he began confidential acquisition talks with one of the Swedish corporation's competitors, a much smaller and technically less sophisticated company. Because the negotiations were too complex for him to handle alone, he circumvented the vice presidents who would have opposed the move and secretly enlisted the help of their subordinates. By the time the negotiations became public, it was too late for the senior staff to stop the deal. The Swedish company canceled its license, and the U.S. company has not sold a single piece of new technology since the acquisition.

This CEO made a grave error in letting his personal feelings interfere with his business judgment, but his incompetence, however great, is not the point. The point is that certain employees concealed information from their immediate superiors. Their motives are easy to guess at and perhaps understandable – after all, they were acting on orders from the CEO. But the fact remains that not one of them spoke up, their superiors suspected nothing, and the consequences for the company were extremely negative.

In these days of mergers and acquisitions, political infighting is often acute after absorption of – or by – another company. Restructuring and consolidation can produce epidemic fear and rupture lines of communication, as this case illustrates:

☐ My electronics corporation acquired a division of another company and merged it with two existing subsidiaries. Many employees were let go in the process of the merger and consolidation. I was named president and CEO of the new company one year after its formation. The new company had its headquarters on the East Coast and its research facilities

> **Mergers, acquisitions, and office politics can all choke off the flow of essential information.**

in the West. The VP for research – whose office was in California – did not tell me that the merger, the layoffs, and the new company policies and procedures had had a terrible impact on employee morale. I was completely unaware of the problem for four months.

Then I visited the research facility to announce a new benefits package. After announcing the plan, I asked for questions. All hell broke loose. For the next year and a half I spent about a third of my time and a great deal of other people's time trying to build bridges and establish trust, hoping to lower turnover, improve productivity, and get those Californians to feel like part of the total company.

Why wasn't I told? My guess is that the subordinate who kept me in the dark was afraid for his own job. Or else he felt he had something to gain by undermining my position. I don't know, but it was an expensive failure of communication.

Building and Destroying Trust

Given the natural obstacles to trust and candor – fear, pride, politics, dislike – managers need to make the most of whatever opportunities they have to increase subordinates' trust. Trust is not easy to build in the best of cases, and the kind of trust that concerns us here has to grow on rocky ground – between people at different levels of authority.

The factors affecting the development of trust and candor fall into six categories: communication, support, respect, fairness, predictability, and competence.

Communication is a matter of keeping subordinates informed, providing accurate feedback, explaining decisions and policies, being candid about one's own problems, and resisting the temptation to hoard information for use as a tool or a reward.

For several years, the founder and CEO of a small, South American conglomerate had addressed the needs of each of his six divisions separately. He treated his vice presidents like the CEOs of the divisions, cutting deals with each of them independently and keeping each in the dark about his arrangements with the others. He had always solved problems on this ad hoc basis, and it worked reasonably well. The company had grown swiftly and steadily. But now times were tougher, the company was bigger, and he began getting complaints from his VPs about resource allocation. None of them was satisfied with his own division's share, but none was in a position to consider the needs of the company as a whole.

At this point, the CEO recognized that his way of managing was part of the problem, did an abrupt about-face, and created an executive committee comprising himself and his six VPs. They all took part in setting priorities, allocating resources, and planning company strategy. Conflicts remained, of course, as each vice president fought for resources for his division. But trust increased substantially, and for the first time there was communication between divisions and a willingness and opportunity for the company's leadership to work together as a team.

Another CEO moved the offices of his small company without notice. His staff simply arrived at work one Monday morning to learn that the movers were coming on Tuesday. When asked to explain, the man gave his reasons but clearly didn't feel his employees needed to know. He insulted and belittled the people he depended on for information and support.

It is important to communicate with subordinates not only as a group but also as individuals. This woman's boss may have believed money spoke for itself:

☐ I have been working for my current boss for two years and never had a performance appraisal. I guess I'm doing okay because I get good raises every year. But I have no idea what the future may hold for me in this company.

Middle- to upper-level managers often find it difficult to talk with superiors about their own perfor-

Resist the temptation to use information as a tool or a reward.

mance and career prospects. When they feel they aren't getting the feedback they need, they are uncomfortable asking for it. Communication must flow in both directions if it is to flow at all. Information won't surge up where it barely trickles down.

Support means showing concern for subordinates as people. It means being available and approachable. It means helping people, coaching them, encouraging their ideas, and defending their positions. It may mean socializing with them. It certainly means taking an interest in their lives and careers. Here are three examples of good and poor support:

☐ During one period of my life, I had some serious personal problems that affected my work. My boss protected me at work and gave me a lot of moral support. Eventually, I was able to solve my problems, thanks in part to her help. That strengthened our professional relationship enormously.
☐ I presented a proposal to the executive committee. Some members were in favor, others against. I was so young and nervous, I didn't see how I could possibly convince them I was right. Then my boss took on the

defense of my proposal, argued energetically in favor of it, and we won. When I think back on it now, I realize that few events in my career have pleased me more or given me a more genuine sense of gratitude.
☐ I approved a credit and had been authorized by my boss to waive certain credit warranties. Then some other people started questioning what I had done and throwing doubt on my competence. Instead of supporting me, my boss took the side of my critics.

It is often tempting to abandon an employee who is in trouble, out of favor, or simply unpopular, but the extra effort expended in behalf of such a person can pay big dividends later. When you have to terminate employees, the worst possible method is to let them twist in the wind. Get rid of those you have to get rid of. Support the others for all you're worth. Subordinates trust most deeply the superiors they feel will stand by them when the chips are down.

Respect feeds on itself. The most important form of respect is delegation, and the second most important is listening to subordinates and acting on their opinions. In the first two examples below, the boss shows genuine respect for the subordinate's judgment and intelligence. In the third, the relationship actually deteriorates in the course of the meeting.

☐ My boss put me in charge of a project. It involved a big risk for me, but an even bigger risk for her if I failed. I asked her how she wanted me to do it and who else I should contact for clearance. She said, "You have free rein on this. Whatever you do is okay with me."
☐ Six years ago, just after I joined the bank, my boss told me he had decided to buy a company and asked me to look into it and give him my opinion. I did my homework and told him I thought it was a bad idea. So he eliminated me from the team he had put together to manage the acquisition. Somehow I succeeded in persuading him to listen to a fuller presentation of my analysis. He not only took the time, he really listened to my arguments and finally canceled the purchase.
☐ My boss and I agreed that we had to reduce the personnel in my department. I wanted to cut five positions; he wanted to cut eight. I argued my case for an hour. In the end he forced me to cut eight jobs, without even answering my arguments, and I realized he hadn't paid attention to anything I'd said.

In interpersonal relations, the law of reciprocity tends to rule. When supervisors use a lot of fine words about trust and respect but behave disdainfully, subordinates are likely to respond in kind.

Fairness means giving credit where it's due, being objective and impartial in performance appraisals, giving praise liberally. The opposite kind of behavior —favoritism, hypocrisy, misappropriating ideas and accomplishments, unethical behavior—is difficult to forgive and hugely destructive of trust. These two examples make the point well:

☐ One of my subordinates had what I thought was a terrific idea, and I told my boss. He agreed and immediately dictated a memo to the division manager outlining the idea and giving full credit where it was due. I learned sometime later that he never sent that memo but substituted another in which he took a good share of the credit for himself—and gave an equal share to me. I not only felt cheated, I felt I had somehow taken part in a plot to cheat the person who had the idea in the first place. It not only destroyed my relationship with that boss, it almost ruined my relationship with my subordinate.

☐ We were involved in a very difficult lawsuit with a former client. The battle lasted four years, and in the end we lost the case before the Supreme Court. When I gave the news to my boss, I was afraid he would take it badly, as a kind of personal failure. But he understood that we lost because of factors completely out of our control, and, instead of criticizing us, he praised our hard work and dedication.

Chronic lack of fairness will dry up trust and candor quickly, but every act of support and fair play will prime the pump.

Predictability is a matter of behaving consistently and dependably and of keeping both explicit and implicit promises. A broken promise can do considerable damage, as this example illustrates:

☐ When my boss hired me, she promised me a percentage of the profits on the project I was to manage. My arrival was delayed, so I took over the project as it

Not giving credit where it's due is hugely destructive of trust.

was winding down—without any profits to speak of. As soon as I cleaned up the loose ends, I took over a new project that was my responsibility from the outset. I managed it well, and profits were substantial. I felt badly cheated when I was told that my percentage deal applied to the first project only, that I had no such agreement on the second. I complained bitterly, and the company made it right. But it left a bad taste in my mouth, and I left shortly afterward.

Another form of predictability is consistency of character, which is, after all, the best proof of authenticity.

Competence, finally, means demonstrating technical and professional ability and good business sense. Employees don't want to be subordinate to people they see as incompetent. Trust grows from seeds of decent behavior, but it thrives on the admiration and respect that only a capable leader can command.

Learning to Recognize Signs of Trouble

Building trust and candor is a gradual process, a long chain of positive experiences: trusting employees with important assignments, publicly defending their positions and supporting their ideas, showing candor and fairness in evaluating their work, and so forth. And because trust takes time to build and has natural limits once achieved, it is easy to destroy. Betraying a confidence, breaking a promise, humiliating an employee in public, lying, withholding information, or excluding subordinates from groups in which they feel they rightly belong—any of these can do instant and irreparable damage to a trust relationship that has taken months or years to develop.

Given these limitations, can managers rely on subordinates to come forward with problems before they become critical?

The obvious answer is no, not entirely. Honest, forthright communication is the best source of information about problems that managers have, and good ones make the most of it. At the same time, they learn to recognize subtle signs of danger, and they develop and refine alternative sources of information to fill in the gaps. My interviews indicate that there are several important warning signs that managers can look for.

Decline in information flow is often a first sign of trouble. Streams of information suddenly go dry. Subordinates communicate less, express opinions reluctantly, avoid discussions—even meetings. Reports are late, subordinates are more difficult to reach, and follow-up has to be more thorough and deliberate. In this example, the first warning was a series of glib reassurances that didn't quite jibe with reality:

☐ I was exploration manager for an oil company in Venezuela. I began to notice that when I asked about one particular project, I got very short and superficial answers assuring me that everything was okay. But there were some contradictory signals. For example, labor turnover in the project was quite high. I had a gut feeling that something was seriously wrong. I contacted the area manager, but he couldn't put his finger on any specific problem. I called the field supervisor and still got no clear answers. I went to the field location and spent two days. Nothing. Then I sent a trustworthy young assistant to work with the field crews for a week, and he uncovered the problem. Local labor subcontractors were bribing the workers, increasing turnover, and taking in a lot of money for supplying replacements. We were not only spending more on labor bounties, we were often working with green hands instead of well-trained workers.

Deterioration of morale can reveal itself in lack of enthusiasm, reduced cooperation, increased complaints about workload, a tendency to dump more minor problems on the boss's desk. At a more advanced stage, absenteeism starts to rise and aggressive behavior—increased criticism, irritability, finger pointing, and the like—appears.

Ambiguous verbal messages come from subordinates who aren't quite comfortable with the information they are passing on. They may be reluctant to blow a potential problem out of proportion, or they may be testing to see if the door is open for a more serious discussion.

In one example, the head of an R&D lab asked the woman in charge of a large research project how a newly hired scientist was working out. The woman said, "He's very bright, but a bit strange. But he's working very hard and is extremely enthusiastic. He's okay." The boss missed the message. "I'm glad everything's okay" was all he said.

In this case, the woman's answer was a typical sign of trouble in sandwich form—positive, negative, positive. The subordinate who answers this way may simply be testing her boss's attention. When he failed to pick up on the "he's a bit strange" remark, she dropped the matter. Her boss never found out that she felt threatened by the scientist's brilliance and that his prima donna behavior made her angry. The friction between them grew, and she eventually took a job with another division.

Nonverbal signals can take a wide variety of forms, from body language to social behavior to changes in routines and habits.

The director of the international division of a major U.S. bank noticed that his chief of Asian operations had begun to work with his office door closed during his frequent visits to New York. This was unusual behavior: he was a gregarious soul, always available for lunch or a chat, and a closed door was out of character.

After two or three such visits, the director invited him to lunch to talk business. After a bottle of good wine, the younger man brought up what was really on his mind. He had heard rumors that his name had come up to head the European division—the most prestigious foreign assignment—and that the director had opposed him. The rumors were wrong. In fact, the bank was looking for someone to take the director's job, as he was about to be promoted, and the Asian operations chief was a prime candidate.

Consciously or unconsciously, the man sent a signal by closing his door. The lunch invitation was a nonthreatening way of finding out what the signal meant. At the time this took place, business had not yet begun to suffer, but more serious trouble might have

"It's a hostile attempt to take the company public!"

erupted if this man had continued to brood over false rumors. This prompt response to a nonverbal signal kept a small problem from growing into a big one.

Body language, incidentally, is easily misinterpreted. Popular books have encouraged many people to believe they are experts, but interpreting body language is risky business. Distress signals may be triggered by events in a person's private life, for example, and have nothing to do with the office. A more prudent approach is to see body language merely as an indication of a potential problem, without jumping to conclusions about what the problem may be.

Outside signals, such as customer complaints and problems spotted by other company divisions, are also clear warnings, but they often come too late. By this time, the trouble has usually reached the stage of impaired results—decreasing productivity, deteriorating quality, dwindling orders, declining numbers. By now the manager has long since failed.

Turning Hints into Information

When experienced managers see changes in the behavior of the people they supervise, they do their best to amplify hints and gather supplemental information.

As I pointed out at the beginning of this article, by far the easiest way of obtaining information is to get it from a subordinate, in plain English. Managers who have built good relationships with their subordinates often rely on this method. When they see the early warning signs of trouble, they ask questions.

As I have stressed, the answers to their questions will be only as honest as subordinates want to and dare to give. In other words, successful questioning depends partly on the level of trust. However, it also depends partly on a manager's ability to peel away superficial and sometimes misleading symptoms, much like the outside layers of an onion. Effective managers have good clinical sense. This man, for example, had a gut feeling that he had not yet reached the core of the problem:

□ My department was responsible for trade with the Far East, and I needed a good manager for China. I found what I thought was the perfect man. He not only knew all the traders but also spoke fluent English, French, Chinese, and Japanese. The new position was a promotion for him in terms of title and meant a big salary increase.

For the first year, he worked hard, things went well, and we made a lot of money. At the same time, he started to complain about his salary, arguing that

other managers reporting to me and doing the same kind of work were getting 20% more—which was true. I told him he'd already had a 25% increase and that if he continued doing well, he could expect further raises over the next couple of years.

Then I began hearing his complaint from third parties all over the Far East. I discussed the matter with him many times, and eventually his salary rose to within 5% of the other managers. But something was still wrong. Then he suddenly got sick and disappeared from the office for two weeks. When he returned, his opening words were about salary.

Over the next couple of months, however, his health continued to deteriorate, and I began to wonder if salary was the real problem after all. I had several long talks with him and finally learned the truth. His deteriorating health was related to the job and the level of responsibility, which was too great for him to handle. He was so anxious that he couldn't sleep and was having problems with his family. As soon as we both understood the cause of his problem, I promised him a different job with less stress and frustration. He immediately became more relaxed and happier with his salary and his life.

The salary issue was only a symptom—a particularly misleading one, since the man was in fact underpaid by comparison with his colleagues. Notice also the escalation of symptoms from complaints to illness and the fact that it took the narrator several discussions to get at the actual truth. His persistence grew from a gut feeling that salary was not the real problem but rather a masking symptom.

> The best, the most common, and the hardest way of getting information is face to face, in plain English.

When conflicts arise between superiors and subordinates, the most common method of punishing the boss is to withhold information. So the greater the conflict is, the less effective direct questioning will be. Furthermore, if an honest answer means pointing out some of the boss's own shortcomings, almost anyone will think twice.

One way of circumventing this difficulty is to design anonymous forms of communication—suggestion boxes, questionnaires, and performance appraisals of managers by the people who work for them.

One manager took advantage of an odd condition in his office space to coax anonymous information from his staff. The offices were on the ninth and tenth floors of an office building and had two elevators of their own, which every employee rode several times a day. The boss put a bulletin board in each of them and posted frequent notices, including a weekly newsletter about office activities, personnel changes, and industry developments. He then let it be known informally that the bulletin boards were open to everyone—no approvals required—and when the first employee notices appeared, he made a point of leaving them in place for a full week. There were only two rules. First, no clippings from newspapers and magazines—contributions had to be original. Second, nothing tasteless or abusive—but complaints and bellyaching were okay.

The bulletin boards flourished, partly because most people had at least an occasional chance to ride alone and post their own views in private. For a while, there was even an anonymous weekly newspaper that handed out praise and criticism pretty

> ## Using information properly is largely a matter of not *misusing* it.

freely and irreverently. It made some people uncomfortable, but it had no more avid reader than the boss, who learned volumes about the problems and views of his staff and organization.

Criticizing the boss's managerial style and professional competence is probably the hardest thing for employees to do. Remember two critical points: First, top performers are the most likely to feel secure enough to criticize, so ask them first. Second, many of your subordinates have learned the hard way that

honest negative feedback can be dangerous. Never ask for it unless you are certain you can handle it.

Building Information Networks

There are big differences between consuming, disseminating, and creating information. Effective managers seem to have a talent for all three.

Using information well is primarily a matter of not *misusing* it—of being discreet about its sources, of using it not as a weapon but only as a means of solving problems and improving the quality of work life.

Spreading information well means not spreading gossip but also not hoarding the truth. People in organizations want—and have a right to—information that will help them do their jobs better or otherwise affect their lives. In general, they also work better and suffer less stress and fewer complications when they are well informed. At the same time—and more important for this discussion—information attracts information. Managers who are generous with what they know seem to get as much as they give.

Creating information, finally, is a question of assembling scattered facts and interpreting them for others. Shaping data in this way is a skill that needs exercise. It is an act of education and, of course, an act of control.

The final positive outcome for information-rich individuals is that information flows to them as well as away from them. This ability to attract, create, and disseminate information can become an immense managerial asset, a self-perpetuating information network, and a means of creating the trust that the upward flow of candid information depends on.   ▽

MANAGEMENT COMMUNICATION
and the Grapevine

❡ No administrator in his right mind would ever try to abolish the management grapevine. It is as permanent as humanity is. It should be recognized, analyzed, and consciously used for better communication.

By Keith Davis

Communication is involved in all human relations. It is the "nervous system" of any organized group, providing the information and understanding necessary for high productivity and morale. For the individual company it is a continuous process, a way of life, rather than a one-shot campaign. Top management, therefore, recognizes the importance of communication and wants to do something about it. But what? Often, in its frustration, management has used standard communication "packages" instead of dealing situationally with its individual problems. Or it has emphasized the means (communication techniques) rather than the ends (objectives of communication).

One big factor which management has tended to overlook is communication *within its own group*. Communication to the worker and from the worker is dependent on effective management communication; and clearly this in turn requires informal as well as formal channels.

The Grapevine

A particularly neglected aspect of management communication concerns that informal channel, the grapevine. There is no dodging the fact that, as a carrier of news and gossip among executives and supervisors, the grape-

vine often affects the affairs of management. The proof of this is the strong feelings that different executives have about it. Some regard the grapevine as an evil — a thorn in the side which regularly spreads rumor, destroys morale and reputations, leads to irresponsible actions, and challenges authority. Some regard it as a good thing because it acts as a safety valve and carries news fast. Others regard it as a very mixed blessing.

Whether the grapevine is considered an asset or a liability, it is important for executives to try to understand it. For one thing is sure: although no executive can absolutely control the grapevine, he can *influence* it. And since it is here to stay, he should learn to live with it.

Perspective

Of course, the grapevine is only part of the picture of communication in management. There is also formal communication — via conferences, reports, memoranda, and so on; this provides the basic core of information, and many administrators rely on it almost exclusively because they think it makes their job simpler to have everything reduced to explicit terms — as if that were possible! Another important part of the picture is the expression of attitudes, as contrasted with the transmission of information (which is what we will be dealing with in this article). Needless to say, all these factors influence the way the grapevine works in a given company, just as the grapevine in turn influences them.

In this article I want to examine (a) the significance, character, and operation of management communication patterns, with particular emphasis on the grapevine; and (b) the influence that various factors, such as organization and the chain of procedure, have upon such patterns. From this analysis, then, it will be possible to point up (c) the practical implications for management.

As for the research basis of the analysis, the major points are these:

1. *Company studied* — The company upon which the research is based is a real one. I shall refer to it as the "Jason Company." A manufacturer of leather goods, it has 67 people in the management group (that is, all people who supervise the work of others, from top executives to foremen) and about 600 employees. It is located in a rural town of 10,000 persons, and its products are distributed nationally.

In my opinion, the pattern of management communication at the Jason Company is typical of that in many businesses; there were no special conditions likely to make the executives and supervisors act differently from their counterparts in other companies. But let me emphasize that this is a matter of judgment, and hence broader generalizations cannot be made until further research is undertaken.

As a matter of fact, one of the purposes of this article is to encourage businessmen to take a close look at management communication in their own companies and to decide for themselves whether it is the same or different. In many companies, men in the management group now follow the popular practice of examining and discussing their problems of communicating with workers, but rarely do they risk the embarrassment of appraising their communications with each other.

2. *Methodology* — The methods used to study management communication in the Jason Company are new ones. Briefly, the basic approach was to learn from each communication recipient how he first received a given piece of information and then to trace it back to its source. Suppose D and E said they received it from G; G said he received it from B; and B from A. All the chains or sequences were plotted in this way — A to B to G to D and E — and when the data from all recipients were assembled, the pattern of the flow of communication emerged. The findings could be verified and developed further with the help of other data secured from the communication recipients.

This research approach, which I have called "ecco analysis," is discussed in detail elsewhere.[1]

Significant Characteristics

In the Jason Company many of the usual grapevine characteristics were found along with others less well known. For purposes of this discussion, the four most significant characteristics are these:

1. *Speed of transmission* — Traditionally the grapevine is fast, and this showed up in the Jason Company.

For example, a certain manager had an addition to his family at the local hospital at 11 o'clock at night, and by 2:00 p.m. the next day 46% of the whole management group knew about the event. The news was transmitted only by grapevine and mostly by face-to-face conversation, with an occasional interoffice telephone call. Most communications occurred immediately before work began, during "coffee hour," and during lunch hour. The five staff executives who knew of the event learned of it during "coffee hour," indicating that the morning rest period performed an important social function for the staff as well as providing relaxation.

2. *Degree of selectivity* — It is often said that the grapevine acts without conscious direction or thought — that it will carry anything, any time, anywhere. This viewpoint has been epitomized in the statement that "the grapevine is without conscience or consciousness." But flagrant grapevine irresponsibility was not evident in the Jason Company. In fact, the grapevine here showed that it could be highly selective and discriminating.

For example, the local representative of the company which carried the employee group insurance contract planned a picnic for company executives. The Jason Company president decided to invite 36 executives, mostly from higher executive levels. The grapevine immediately went to work spreading this information, but it was carried to *only two of the 31 executives not invited*. The grapevine communicators thought the news was confidential, so they had told only those who they thought would be invited (they had to guess, since they did not have access to the invitation list). The two uninvited executives who knew the information were foremen who were told by their invited superintendent; he had a very close working relationship with them and generally kept them well informed.

Many illustrations like the above could be gathered to show that the grapevine can be discriminating. Whether it may be *counted on* in that respect,

[1] Keith Davis, "A Method of Studying Communication Patterns in Organizations," to be published in *Personnel Psychology*, Fall 1953.

however, is another question. The answer would of course differ with each case and would depend on many variables, including other factors in the communication picture having to do with attitudes, executive relationships, and so forth.

3. *Locale of operation* — The grapevine of company news operates mostly at the place of work.

Jason managers were frequently in contact with each other after work because the town is small; yet grapevine communications about company activities predominantly took place at the plant, rather than away from it. It was at the plant that executives and supervisors learned, for instance, that the president was taking a two weeks' business trip, that the style designer had gone to Florida to study fashion trends, and that an executive had resigned to begin a local insurance business.

The significance of at-the-company grapevines is this: since management has some control over the work environment, it has an opportunity to influence the grapevine. By exerting such influence the manager can more closely integrate grapevine interests with those of the formal communication system, and he can use it for effectively spreading more significant items of information than those commonly carried.

4. *Relation to formal communication* — Formal and informal communication systems tend to be jointly active, or jointly inactive. Where formal communication was inactive at the Jason Company, the grapevine did not rush in to fill the void (as has often been suggested [2]); instead, there simply was lack of communication. Similarly, where there was effective formal communication, there was an active grapevine.

Informal and formal communication may supplement each other. Often formal communication is simply used to confirm or to expand what has already been communicated by grapevine. Thus in the case of the picnic, as just described, management issued formal invitations even to those who already knew they were invited. This necessary process of confirmation results partly because of the speed of the grapevine, which formal systems fail to match, partly because of its unofficial function, and partly because of its transient nature. Formal communication needs to come along to stamp "Official" on the news and to put it "on the record," which the grapevine cannot suitably do.

Spreading Information

Now let us turn to the actual operation of the grapevine. How is information passed along?

What is the relationship among the various people who are involved?

Human communication requires at least two persons, but each person acts independently. Person A may talk or write, but he has not *communicated* until person B receives. The individual is, therefore, a basic communication unit. That is, he is one "link" in the communication "chain" for any bit of information.

EXHIBIT I. TYPES OF COMMUNICATION CHAINS

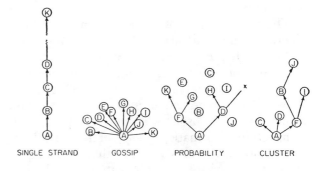

SINGLE STRAND   GOSSIP   PROBABILITY   CLUSTER

The formal communication chain is largely determined by the chain of command or by formal procedures, but the grapevine chain is more flexible. There are four different ways of visualizing it, as EXHIBIT I indicates:

1. *The single-strand chain* — A tells B, who tells C, who tells D, and so on; this makes for a tenuous chain to a distant receiver. Such a chain is usually in mind when one speaks of how the grapevine distorts and filters information until the original item is not recognizable.

2. *The gossip chain* — A seeks and tells everyone else.

3. *The probability chain* — A communicates randomly, say, to F and D, in accordance with the laws of probability; then F and D tell others in the same manner.

4. *The cluster chain* — A tells three selected others; perhaps one of them tells two others; and then one of these two tells one other. This was virtually the only kind of chain found in the Jason Company, and may well be the normal one in industry generally.

Active Minority

The predominance of the cluster chain at the Jason Company means that only a few of the persons who knew a unit of information ever transmitted it — what Jacobson and Seashore call the "liaison" individuals.[3] All others who

[2] For example, see National Industrial Conference Board, *Communicating with Employees*, Studies in Personnel Policy, No. 129 (New York, 1952), p. 34.

[3] Eugene Jacobson and Stanley E. Seashore, "Communication Practices in Complex Organizations," *The Journal of Social Issues*, Vol. VII, No. 3, 1951, p. 37.

received the information did not transmit it; they acted merely as passive receivers.

For example, when a quality-control problem occurred, 68% of the executives received the information, but only 20% transmitted it. Again, when an executive planned to resign to enter the insurance business, 81% of the executives knew about it, but only 11% passed the news on to others. Those liaison individuals who told the news to more than one other person amounted to less than 10% of the 67 executives in each case.

These active groups varied in membership. There was no evidence that any one group consistently acted as liaison persons; instead, different types of information passed through different liaison persons. However, as will be shown later, some individuals were invariably communication "isolates"; they received and transmitted information poorly or not at all.

The above findings indicate that if management wants more communication, it should increase the number and/or effectiveness of its liaison individuals. This appears to be a large order, but it is entirely possible. Liaison individuals tend to act in a predictable way. If an individual's unit of information concerns a job function in which he is interested, he is likely to tell others. If his information is about a person with whom he is associated socially, he also is likely to tell others. Furthermore, the sooner he knows of an event after it happened, the more likely he is to tell others. If he gets the information late, he does not want to advertise his late receipt of it by telling it to others.

In other words, three well-known communication principles which are so often mentioned in relation to attitudes also have a major influence on the spread of information by liaison individuals:

(1) Tell people about what will affect them (job interest).

(2) Tell people what they want to know, rather than simply what you want them to know (job and social interest).

(3) Tell people soon (timing).

Organizational Effects

The way an organization is divided horizontally into organizational levels and vertically into functions, such as production and sales, obviously has effects on management communication, for it cuts each company's over-all administrative function into small work assignments, or jobs, and sets each management person in certain relationships to others in his company.

Horizontal Levels

Organizational levels are perhaps the more dramatic in effect because they usually carry authority, pay increases, and status. From the communication point of view, they are especially important because of their number. In a typical firm there are usually several management levels, but only one or two worker levels; furthermore, as the firm grows, the management levels increase in number, while the worker levels remain stationary.

Communication problems are aggravated by these additional levels because the chain of communication is lengthened and complicated. Indeed, just because of this, some companies have been led to try to reduce the number of intermediate management levels. Our concern here is with the patterns of communication among individuals at the different levels.

At the Jason Company, executives at *higher* levels communicated more often and with more people than did executives at *lower* levels. In other words, the predominant communication flow was downward or horizontal. When an event happened at the bottom level, usually the news did reach a high level; but a single line of communication sufficed to carry it there, and from that point it went downward and outward in the same volume and manner (cluster chain) as if it had originated at the top.

Accordingly, the higher an executive was in the organizational hierarchy (with the exception of nonresident executives), the greater was his knowledge of company events. This was true of events which happened both above his level and below his level. Thus, if the president was out of town, a greater proportion at the fourth level knew of it than at the sixth level. Or — and this is less to be expected — if a foreman at the sixth level had an accident, a larger proportion of executives at the third level knew of it than at the fourth level, or even than at the sixth level where the accident happened. The more noteworthy the event, of course, the more likely it was to be known at upper levels — but, in a company of this size, it had to be quite trivial indeed before it failed to reach the ears of top executives.

The converse follows that in terms of communications transmitted and received the sixth and lowest level of supervision, the foreman level, was largely isolated from all other management. The average foreman was very hesitant to communicate with other members of management; and on the rare occasions when he did, he usually chose someone at his own level and preferably in his own department. Members of this group tended to be the last links in management communication, regardless of whether the chains were formal or informal.

A further significant fact concerns the eight departmental superintendents at the fourth level. Six of them supervised foremen directly; two others, with larger departments, each had a single line assistant between him and his foremen. The two who had line assistants were much more active in the communication chains than were the six others; indeed, all but one of the six appeared to have little to do with their foremen except in a formal way.

Perhaps the clue is that, with increased organizational levels, those at the higher (and hence further removed) levels both recognize a greater need for communication and have more time to practice it!

Functional Groups

Functionalization, the second important way in which an organization is "cut up," also has a significant impact on communication in management. The functions which are delegated to a manager help to determine the people he contacts, his relationships with them, his status, and, as a result, the degree to which he receives and transmits information. More specifically, his role in communication is affected (a) by his position in the chain of command and (b) by his position in the chain of procedure, which involves the sequence of work performance and cuts across chains of command, as when a report goes from the superintendent in one chain of command to the chief engineer in another chain of command and to the controller in still another.

In the Jason Company the effects of functionalization showed up in three major ways:

1. *Staff men "in the know"* — More staff executives than line men usually knew about any company event. This was true at each level of management as well as for the management group as a whole. For example, when the president of the company made a trip to seek increased governmental allotments of hides to keep the line tannery operating at capacity, only 4% of the line

executives knew the purpose of the trip, but 25% of the staff men did. In another case, when a popular line superintendent was awarded a hat as a prize in a training program for line superintendents, within six days a larger proportion of the staff executives than of the line executives knew about this event.

The explanation is not just that, with one staff executive to every three line executives, there were more line executives to be informed. More important is the fact that the *chain of procedure* usually involved more staff executives than line executives. Thus, when the superintendent was awarded his hat, a line executive had approved the award, but a staff personnel executive had processed it and a staff accounting executive had arranged for the special check.

Also the staff was more *mobile* than the line. Staff executives in such areas as personnel and control found that their duties both required and allowed them to get out of their offices, made it easy for them to walk through other departments without someone wondering whether they were "not working," to get away for coffee, and so on — all of which meant they heard more news from the other executives they talked with. (In a larger company staff members might be more fixed to their chairs, but the situation in the Jason Company doubtless applies to a great many other businesses.)

Because of its mobility and its role in the chain of procedure, the staff not only received but also transmitted communications more actively than did the line. Most of these communications were oral; at least in this respect, the staff was not the "paper mill" it is often said to be. It seems obvious that management would do well to make conscious use of staff men as communicators.

2. *Cross-communication* — A second significant effect of functionalization in the Jason Company was that the predominant flow of information for events of general interest was between the four large areas of production, sales, finance and office, and industrial relations, rather than within them. That is, if a production executive had a bit of news of general interest, he was more likely to tell a sales, finance, or personnel executive than another production executive.

Social relationships played a part in this, with executives in the various groups being lodge brothers, members of the same church, neighbors, parents of children in the same schools, and so on. In these relationships the desire to make an impression was a strong motivation for cross-communication, since imparting information to executives outside his own area served to make a man feel that the others would consider him "in the know."

Procedural relationships, discussed earlier, also encouraged the executives to communicate across functional lines.

Since communications tended not to stay within an area, such as production, they tended even less to follow chains of command from boss to sub-boss to sub-sub-boss. Indeed, the chain of command was seldom used in this company except for very formal communications. Thus Exhibit II reproduces a communication chain concerning a quality control problem in production, first brought to the attention of a group sales manager in a letter from a customer. Although it was the type of problem that could have been communicated along the chain of command, the exhibit shows that, of 14 communications, only 3 were within the chain of command and only 6 remained within one functional area — sales — where the information was first received.

chains. Also, there were other groups which received information but did not transmit it, and thus contributed to the same problem — the uneven spread of information through the company. Here are three examples at the foreman level illustrating different degrees of failure to participate in the communication process and different reasons for this failure:

(a) The foremen in one group were generally left out of communication chains. These men were of a different nationality from that of the rest of the employees, performed dirty work, and worked in a separate building. Also, their work fitted into the manufacturing process in such a way that it was seldom necessary for other executives to visit their work location.

(b) Another group often was in a communication chain but on the tail end of it. They were in a separate building some distance from the main

EXHIBIT II. COMMUNICATION CHAIN FOR A QUALITY CONTROL PROBLEM

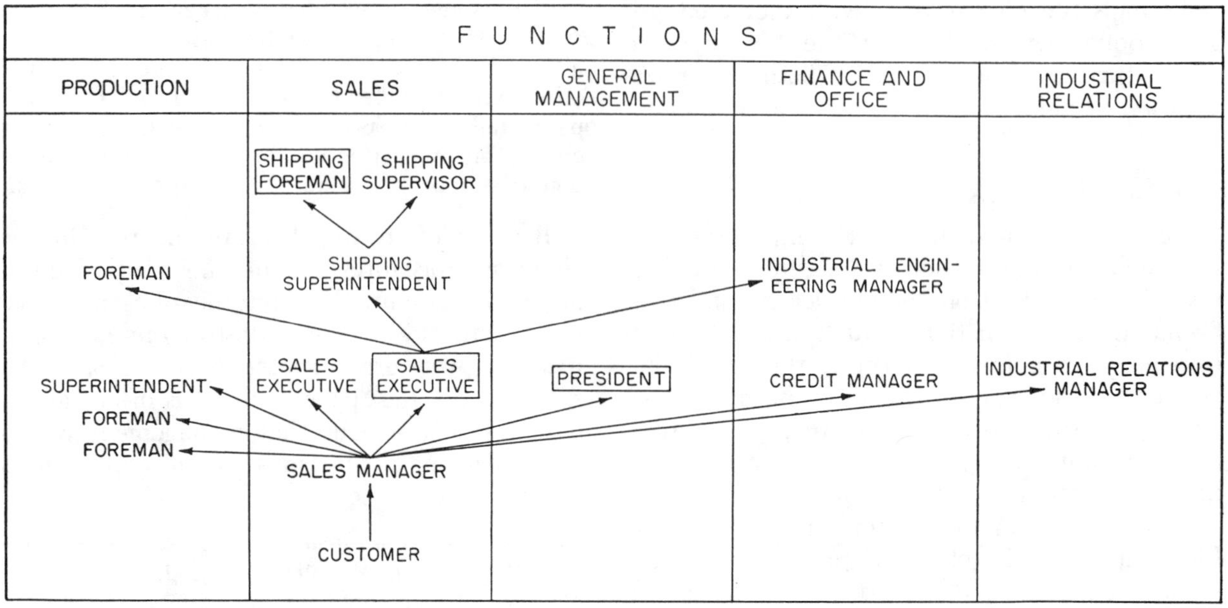

NOTE: Executives in boxes received chain-of-command communications.

The fact that the chain of command may affect management communication patterns less than procedural and social influences — which has shown up in other companies too [4] — means that management needs to devote considerably more attention to the problems and opportunities of cross-communication.

3. *Group isolation* — The research in the Jason Company revealed that some functional groups were consistently isolated from communication

[4] See Carroll L. Shartle, "Leadership and Executive Performance," *Personnel*, March 1949, pp. 377-378.

manufacturing area, their function was not in the main manufacturing procedure, and they usually received information late. They had little chance or incentive to communicate to other executives.

(c) A third group both received and transmitted information, but transmitted only within a narrow radius. Although they were in the midst of the main work area, they failed to communicate with other functional groups because their jobs required constant attention and they felt socially isolated.

In sum, the reasons for group isolation at the Jason Company were: geographical separation; work association (being outside the main procedures or at the end of them); social isolation; and organizational level (the lower the level of a group, the greater its tendency to be isolated).

Obviously, it is not often feasible for management to undertake to remove such causes of group isolation as geographical or social separation. On the other hand, it may well be possible to compensate for them. For example, perhaps the volume of formal communication to men who happen to be in a separate building can be increased, or arrangements can be made for a coffee break that will bring men who are isolated because of the nature of their work or their nationality into greater contact with other supervisors. In each situation management should be able to work out measures that would be appropriate to the individual circumstances.

Conclusion

The findings at the Jason Company have yet to be generalized by research in other industries, but they provide these starting points for action:

(1) If management wants more communication among executives and supervisors, one way is to increase the number and effectiveness of the liaison individuals.

(2) It should count on staff executives to be more active than line executives in spreading information.

(3) It should devote more attention to cross-communication — that is, communication between men in different departments. It is erroneous to consider the chain of command as *the* communication system because it is only one of many influences. Indeed, procedural and social factors are even more important.

(4) It should take steps to compensate for the fact that some groups are "isolated" from communication chains.

(5) It should encourage further research about management grapevines in order to provide managers with a deeper understanding of them and to find new ways of integrating grapevine activities with the objectives of the firm.

(6) "Ecco analysis," the recently developed research approach used at the Jason Company, should be useful for future studies.

If management wants to do a first-class communication job, at this stage it needs fewer medicines and more diagnoses. Communication analysis has now passed beyond "pure research" to a point where it is immediately useful to top management in the individual firm. The patterns of communication that show up should serve to indicate both the areas where communication is most deficient and the channels through which information can be made to flow most effectively.

In particular, no administrator in his right mind would try to abolish the management grapevine. It is as permanent as humanity is. Nevertheless, many administrators have abolished the grapevine from *their own minds*. They think and act without giving adequate weight to it or, worse, try to ignore it. This is a mistake. The grapevine is a factor to be reckoned with in the affairs of management. The administrator should analyze it and should consciously try to influence it.

Skilled incompetence

Chris Argyris

"Managers who are skilled communicators may also be good at covering up real problems."

The ability to get along with others is always an asset, right? Wrong. By adeptly avoiding conflict with coworkers, some executives eventually wreak organizational havoc. And it's their very adeptness that's the problem. The explanation for this lies in what I call skilled incompetence, whereby managers use practiced routine behavior (skill) to produce what they do not intend (incompetence). We can see this happen when managers talk to each other in ways that are seemingly candid and straightforward. What we don't see so clearly is how managers' skills can become institutionalized and create disastrous side effects in their organizations. Consider this familiar situation:

The entrepreneur-CEO of a fast-growing medium-sized company brought together his bright, dedicated, hardworking top managers to devise a new strategic plan. The company had grown at about 45% per year, but fearing that it was heading into deep administrative trouble, the CEO had started to rethink his strategy. He decided he wanted to restructure his organization along more rational, less ad hoc, lines. As he saw it, the company was split between the sales-oriented people who sell off-the-shelf products and the people producing custom services who are oriented toward professionals. And each group was suspicious of the other. He wanted the whole group to decide what kind of company it was going to run.

His immediate subordinates agreed that they must develop a vision and make some strategic decisions. They held several long meetings to do this. Although the meetings were pleasant enough and no

Chris Argyris is the James Bryant Conant Professor of Education and Organizational Behavior at the Harvard University Graduate School of Education. His studies have focused on how people learn and have resulted in a long list of articles—many of which have appeared in HBR—and books, the latest of which is Strategy, Change, and Defensive Routines (Ballinger, 1985).

one seemed to be making life difficult for anyone else, they concluded with no agreements or decisions. "We end up compiling lists of issues but not deciding," said one vice president. Another added, "And it gets pretty discouraging when this happens every time we meet." A third worried aloud, "If you think we are discouraged, how do you think the people below us feel who watch us repeatedly fail?"

This is a group of executives who are at the top, who respect each other, who are highly committed, and who agree that developing a vision and strategy is critical. Yet whenever they meet, they fail to create the vision and the strategy they desire. What is going on here? Are the managers really so incompetent? If so, why?

What causes incompetence

At first, the executives in the previous example believed that they couldn't formulate and implement a good strategic plan because they lacked sound financial data. So they asked the financial vice president to reorganize and reissue the data. Everyone agreed he did a superb job.

But the financial executive reported to me, "Our problem is *not* the absence of financial data. I can flood them with data. We lack a vision of what kind of company we want to be and a strategy. Once we produce those, I can supply the necessary data." The other executives reluctantly agreed.

After several more meetings in which nothing got done, a second explanation emerged. It had to do with the personalities of the individuals and the way they work with each other. The CEO explained, "This is a group of lovable guys with very strong egos. They are competitive, bright, candid, and dedicated. But when we meet, we seem to go in circles; we are not prepared to give in a bit and make the necessary compromises."

Is this explanation valid? Should the top managers become less competitive? I'm not sure. Some management groups are not good at problem solving and decision making precisely because the participants have weak egos and are uncomfortable with competition.

If personality were really the problem, the cure would be psychotherapy. And it's simply not true that to be more effective, executives need years on the couch. Besides, pinpointing personality as the issue hides the real culprit.

The culprit is skill

Let's begin by asking whether counterproductive behavior is also natural and routine. Does everyone seem to be acting sincerely? Do things go wrong even though the managers are not being destructively manipulative and political?

For the executive group, the answer to these questions is yes. Their motives were decent, and they were at their personal best. Their actions were spontaneous, automatic, and unrehearsed. They acted in milliseconds; they were skilled communicators.

How can skillful actions be counterproductive? When we're skillful we usually produce what we intend. So, in a sense, did the executives. In this case, the skilled behavior – the spontaneous and automatic responses – was meant to avoid upset and conflict at the meetings. The unintended by-products are what cause trouble. Because the executives don't say what they really mean or test the assumptions they really hold, their skills inhibit a resolution of the important intellectual issues embedded in developing the strategy. Thus the meetings end with only lists and no decisions.

This pattern of failure is not only typical for this group of managers. It happens to people in all kinds of organizations regardless of age, gender, educational background, wealth, or position in the hierarchy. Let me illustrate with another example that involves the entire organizational culture at the upper levels. Here we'll begin to see how people's tendency to avoid conflict, to duck the tough issues, becomes institutionalized and leads to a culture that can't tolerate straight talk.

Where the skillful thrive

The top management of a large, decentralized corporation was having difficulty finding out what some of its division presidents were up to. Time and time again the CEO would send memos to the presidents asking for information, and time and time again they'd send next to nothing in return. But other people at headquarters accepted this situation as normal. When asked why they got so little direct communication from their division heads, they'd respond, "That's the way we do things around here."

Here is an organization that isn't talking to itself. The patterns that managers set up among themselves have become institutionalized, and what were once characteristic personal exchanges have now become organizational defensive routines. Before I go on to describe what these routines look like, let's look at how this situation arose.

Built into decentralization is the age-old tug between autonomy and control: superiors want no surprises, subordinates want to be left alone. The subordinates push for autonomy; they assert that by leaving them alone, top management will show its trust from a distance. The superiors, on the other hand, try to keep control through information systems. The subordinates see the control devices as confirming their suspicions – their superiors don't trust them.

Many executives I have observed handle this tension by pretending that the tension is not there. They act as if everyone were in accord and trust that no one will point out disagreements and thereby rock the boat. At the same time, however, they do feel the tension and can't help but soft-pedal their talk. They send mixed messages. (See the insert on chaos.)

The CEO in this example kept saying to his division presidents, "I mean it – you run the show down there." The division presidents, wanting to prove their mettle, believed him until an important issue came up. When it did the CEO, concerned about the situation and forgetting that he wanted his division chiefs to be innovative, would make phone calls and send memos seeking information.

Defensive routines emerge

One of the most powerful ways people deal with potential embarrassment is to create "organizational defensive routines." I define these as any action or policy designed to avoid surprise, embarrassment, or threat. But they also prevent learning and

Four easy steps to chaos

How does a manager send mixed messages? It takes skill. Here are four rules:

1
Design a clearly ambiguous message. For example, "Be innovative and take risks, but be careful" is a message that says in effect, "Go, but go just so far" without specifying how far far is. The ambiguity and imprecision cover the speaker who can't know ahead of time what is too far.

The receiver, on the other hand, clearly understands the ambiguity and imprecision. Moreover, he or she knows that a request for more precision would likely be interpreted as a sign of immaturity or inexperience. And the receivers may also need an out some day and may want to keep the message imprecise and ambiguous. Receivers don't want "far" defined any more clearly than the senders do.

2
Ignore any inconsistencies in the message. When people send mixed messages, they usually do it spontaneously and with no sign that the message is mixed. Indeed, if they did appear to hesitate, they would defeat their purpose of maintaining control. Even worse, they might appear weak.

3
Make the ambiguity and inconsistency in the message undiscussable. The whole point of sending a mixed message is to avoid dealing with a situation straight on. The sender does not want the message's mixedness exposed. An executive is not about to send a mixed message and then ask, "Do you find my message inconsistent and ambiguous?" The executive also renders the message undiscussable by the very natural way of sending it. To challenge the innocence of the sender is to imply that the sender is duplicitous—not a likely thing for a subordinate to do.

4
Make the undiscussability also undiscussable. One of the best ways to do this is to send the mixed message in a setting that is not conducive to open inquiry, such as a large meeting or a group where people of unequal organizational status are present. No one wants to launder linen in public. While they are sending mixed messages during a meeting, people rarely reflect on their actions or talk about how the organizational culture, including the meeting, makes discussing the undiscussable difficult.

thereby prevent organizations from investigating or eliminating the underlying problems.

Defensive routines are systemic in that most people within the company adhere to them. People leave the organization and new ones arrive, yet the defensive routines remain intact.

To see the impact of the defensive routines and the range of their effects, let's return to the division heads who are directed by mixed messages. They feel a lack of trust and are suspicious of their boss's intentions but they must, nonetheless, find ways to live with the mixed messages. So they "explain" the messages to themselves and to their subordinates. These explanations often sound like this:

> "Corporate never *really* meant decentralization."

> "Corporate is willing to trust divisions when the going is smooth, but not when it's rough."

> "Corporate is more concerned about the stock market than about us."

Of course, the managers rarely test their hypotheses about corporate motives with top executives. If discussing mixed messages among themselves would be uncomfortable, then public testing of the validity of these explanations would be embarrassing.

But now the division heads are in a double bind. On the one hand, if they go along unquestioningly, they may lose their autonomy and their subordinates will see them as having little influence with corporate. On the other, if the division executives do not comply with orders from above, headquarters will think they are recalcitrant, and if noncompliance continues, disloyal.

Top management is in a similar predicament. It senses that division managers have suspicions about headquarters' motives and are covering them up. If headquarters makes its impression known, though, the division heads may get upset. If the top does not say anything, the division presidents could infer full agreement when there is none. Usually, in the name of keeping up good relations, the top covers up its predicament.

Soon, people in the divisions learn to live with their binds by generating further explanations. For example, they may eventually conclude that openness is a strategy that top management has devised intentionally to cover up its unwillingness to be influenced.

Since this conclusion is based on the assumption that people at the top are covering up, managers won't test it either. Since neither headquarters nor division executives discuss or resolve the attributions or the frustrations, both may eventually stop communicating regularly and openly. Once in place, the climate of mistrust makes it more likely that the issues become undiscussable.

Now both headquarters and division managers have attitudes, assumptions, and actions that create self-fulfilling and self-sealing processes that each sees the other as creating.

"It's an interesting invention, but because of some irregularities, the elders have decided to have it recalled."

Under these conditions, it is not surprising to find that superiors and subordinates hold both good and bad feelings about each other. For example, they may say about each other: "They are bright and well intentioned but they have a narrow, parochial view"; or "They are interested in the company's financial health but they do not understand how they are harming earnings in the long run"; or "They are interested in people but they pay too little attention to the company's development."

My experience is that people cannot build on their appreciation of others without first overcoming their suspicions. But to overcome what they don't like, people must be able to discuss it. And this requirement violates the undiscussability rule embedded in the organizational defensive routines.

Is there any organization that does not have these hang-ups and problems? Some people suggest that getting back to basics will open lines of communication. But the proffered panacea does not go far enough; it does not deal with the underlying patterns. Problems won't be solved by simply correcting one isolated instance of poor performance.

When CEOs I have observed declared war against organizational barriers to candor and demanded that people get back to basics, most often they implemented the new ideas with the old skills. People changed whatever they could and learned to cover their asses even more skillfully. The freedom to question and to confront is crucial, but it is inadequate. To overcome skilled incompetence, people have to learn new skills—to ask the questions behind the questions.

Defensive routines exist. They are undiscussable. They proliferate and grow underground. And the social pollution is hard to identify until something occurs that blows things open. Often that something is a glaring error whose results cannot be hidden. The recent space shuttle disaster is an example. Only after the accident occurred were the mixed messages and defensive routines used during the decision to launch exposed. The disaster made it legitimate for outsiders to require insiders to discuss the undiscussable. (By the way, writing a tighter set of controls and requiring better communication won't solve the problem. Tighter controls will only enlarge the book of rules that William Rogers, chairman of the president's committee to investigate the Challenger disaster, acknowledged can be a cure worse than the illness. He pointed out that in his Navy years, when the players went by the book, things only got worse.)

Managers do not have the choice to ignore the organizational problems that these self-sealing loops create. They may be able to get away with it today, but they're creating a legacy for those who will come after them.

How to become unskilled

The top management group I described at the beginning of this article decided to learn new skills by examining the defenses they created in their own meetings.

First, they arranged a two-day session away from the office for which they wrote a short case beforehand. The purpose of these cases was twofold. First, they allowed the executives to develop a collage of the problems they thought were critical. Not surprisingly, in this particular group at least half wrote on issues related to the product versus custom service conflict. Second, the cases provided a kind of window into the prevailing rules and routines the executives used. The form of the case was as follows:

1　In one paragraph describe a key organizational problem as you see it.

2　In attacking the problem, assume you could talk to whomever you wish. Describe, in a paragraph or so, the strategy you would use in this meeting.

3　Next, split your page into two columns. On the right-hand side, write how you would begin the meeting: what you would actually say. Then write what you believe the other(s) would say. Then write your response to their response. Continue writing this scenario for two or so double-spaced typewritten pages.

4   In the left-hand column write any of your ideas or feelings that you would not communicate for whatever reason.

The executives reported that they became engrossed in writing the cases. Some said that the very writing of their case was an eye-opener. Moreover, once the stories were distributed, the reactions were jocular. They enjoyed them: "Great, Joe does this all the time"; "Oh, there's a familiar one"; "All salespeople and no listeners"; "Oh my God, this is us."

What is the advantage of using the cases? Crafted and written by the executives themselves, they become vivid examples of skilled incompetence. They illustrate the skill with which each executive sought to avoid upsetting the other while trying to change the other's mind. The cases also illustrate their incompetence. By their own analysis, what they did upset the others, created suspicion, and made it less likely that their views would prevail.

The cases are also very important learning devices. During a meeting, it is difficult to slow down behavior produced in milliseconds, to reflect on it, and to change it. For one thing, it's hard to pay attention to interpersonal actions and to substantive issues at the same time.

A collage from several cases appears in the *Exhibit*. It was written by executives who believed the company should place a greater emphasis on custom service.

The cases written by individuals who supported the product strategy did not differ much. They too were trying to persuade, sell, or cajole their fellow officers. Their left-hand columns were similar.

In analyzing their left-hand columns, the executives found that each side blamed the other for the difficulties, and they used the same reasons. For example, each side said:

"If you insist on your position, you'll harm the morale I've built."

"Don't hand me that line. You know what I'm talking about."

"Why don't you take off your blinders and wear a company hat?"

"It upsets me when I think of how they think."

"I'm really trying hard, but I'm beginning to feel this is hopeless."

Exhibit	Case of the custom-service advocate

Thoughts and feelings	Actual conversation
He's not going to like this topic, but we have to discuss it. I doubt that he will take a company perspective, but I should be positive.	**I:** Hi Bill. I appreciate having the opportunity to talk with you about this custom service versus product problem. I'm sure that both of us want to resolve it in the best interests of the company.
	Bill: I'm always glad to talk about it, as you well know.
I better go slow. Let me ease in.	**I:** There are a rising number of situations where our clients are asking for custom service and rejecting the off-the-shelf products. I worry that your salespeople will play an increasingly peripheral role in the future.
	Bill: I don't understand. Tell me more.
Like hell you don't understand. I wish there was a way I could be more gentle.	**I:** Bill, I'm sure you are aware of the changes [I explain].
	Bill: No, I don't see it that way. My salespeople are the key to the future.
There he goes, thinking like a salesman and not like a corporate officer.	**I:** Well, let's explore that a bit.

These cases effectively illustrate the influence of skilled incompetence. In crafting the cases, the executives were trying not to upset the others and at the same time were trying to change their minds. This process requires skill. Yet the skill they used in the cases has the unintended side effects I talked about. In the cases, the others became upset and dug in their heels without changing their minds.

Here's a real problem. These executives and all the others I've studied to date can't prevent the counterproductive consequences until and unless they learn new skills. Nor will it work to bypass the skilled incompetence by focusing on the business problems, such as, in this case, developing a business strategy.

The answer is unlearning

The crucial step is for executives to begin to revise how they'd tackle their case. At their two-day seminar each manager selected an episode he wished to redesign so that it would not have the un-happy result it currently produced.

In rewriting their cases, the managers realized that they would have to slow things down. They could not produce a new conversation in the milliseconds in which they were accustomed to speak. This troubled them a bit because they were impatient to learn. They had to keep reminding themselves that learning new skills meant they had to slow down.

Each manager took a different manager's case and crafted a new conversation to help the writer of the episode. After five minutes or so, they showed their designs to the writer. In the process of discussing these new versions, the writer learned a lot about how to redesign his words. And, as they discovered the bugs in their suggestions and the way they made them, the designers also learned a lot.

The dialogues were constructive, cooperative, and helpful. Typical comments were:

> "If you want to reach me, try it the way Joe just said."

> "I realize your intentions are good, but those words push my button."

> "I understand what you're trying to say, but it doesn't work for me. How about trying it this way?"

> "I'm surprised at how much my new phrases contain the old messages. This will take time."

Practice is important. Most people require as much practice to overcome skilled incompetence as to play a not-so-decent game of tennis. But it doesn't need to happen all at once. Once managers are committed to change, the practice can occur in actual business meetings where executives set aside some time to reflect on their actions and to correct them.

But how does unlearning skilled incompetence lead to fewer organizational snafus? The first step is to make sure executives are aware of defensive routines that surround the organizational problems that they are trying to solve. One way to do this is to observe them in the making. For example, during a meeting of the top line and corporate staff officers in our large decentralized organization, the CEO asked why the line and staff were having problems working effectively. They identified at least four causes:

> The organization's management philosophy and policies are inadequate.

> Corporate staff roles overlap and lead to confusion.

> Staff lacks clear-cut authority when dealing with line.

> Staff has inadequate contact with top line officers.

The CEO appointed two task forces to come up with solutions. Several months later, the entire group met for a day and hammered out a solution that was acceptable to all.

This story has two features that I would highlight. First, the staff-line problems are typical. Second, the story has a happy ending. The organization got to the root of its problems.

But there is a question that must be answered in order to get at the organizational defensive routines. Why did all the managers—both upper and lower—adhere to, implement, and maintain inadequate policies and confusing roles in the first place?

Why open this can of worms if we have already solved the problem? Because defensive routines prevent executives from making honest decisions. Managers who are skilled communicators may also be good at covering up real problems. If we don't work hard at reducing defensive routines, they will thrive—ready to undermine this solution and cover up other conflicts. ▽

There is great skill in knowing how to conceal one's skill.

La Rochefoucauld

Overcoming group warfare

How should you go about reconciling the differences between groups that need to cooperate but that already have swords drawn?

Robert R. Blake and Jane S. Mouton

The company you run stands on the threshold of success. The competition's new product has serious flaws, and all you need do to take giant strides toward controlling market share is to hit the market with your new product. Nothing stands in your way except, of course, that pesky misunderstanding between the product design group and manufacturing. They just can't seem to get along, and it does look as if you may have to push the start-up date back a little. You realize suddenly that if the battle between the two groups doesn't end, the product may not get to market in time to take advantage of the space your competitor has left.

What should you do? The authors of this article present two very different approaches to resolving conflicts between embattled groups. In one method, a neutral facilitator tries to mediate between the two groups by offering compromises and trying to get each group to see the other's point of view. In the other method, the groups form their own views of what their ideal relationship should be and a neu-

tral administrator helps them go through steps to achieve it. Examining two cases of conflict in detail, the authors show how the two approaches work, discuss the outsider's role in each, and offer guidelines for deciding when one approach is likely to work better than the other.

Robert R. Blake and Jane S. Mouton are directors of Scientific Research, Inc., a consulting firm located in Austin, Texas. They are well-known for their work in organization development, especially for developing the "managerial grid," which they wrote about with Louis B. Barnes and Larry E. Greiner in HBR exactly 20 years ago in the November-December 1964 issue (see "Breakthrough in Organization Development"). This is their first HBR article since then. It is adapted from their book, Solving Costly Organizational Conflicts: Achieving Intergroup Trust, Cooperation, and Teamwork *(Jossey-Bass, 1984).*

While many people worried about the absence of experienced air traffic controllers after the Professional Air Traffic Controllers Organization went on strike in 1981, they also wondered why it was so difficult for the FAA and PATCO to come to terms before the strike was called. Important groups that need to cooperate can often overcome their difficulties and continue working together, but sometimes they can't. Over the years disputants in the transportation and coal industries have had skirmishes that have resulted in open warfare. Even when the battles are not waged so publicly or fiercely, the human and material costs organizations pay can be staggering.

We have identified two strategies for resolving intergroup conflicts, each with variations. What we have come to call the *interpersonal facilitator approach* relies on a neutral person to provide a bridge to help disputing parties find common ground. The facilitator does this by identifying areas of agreement as well as disagreement so that the latter can be reduced and resolution achieved.

In what we call the *interface conflict-solving approach*, disputants deal with each other directly as members of whole groups. A neutral person helps the groups go through a program of steps that aids principal members of both groups to identify and resolve their differences.

Line managers and internal consultants who are respected and neutral may serve as facilitators or administrators of the step program. The person selected should be of a rank comparable to or higher than that of the highest-ranking member in either of the groups in conflict. A neutral of lesser rank is likely to be brushed aside by a higher-ranking member in a group bent on attack. When the conflict is between headquarters and a subsidiary or when top management is involved in both groups, as in a merger, the groups should consider calling in an outsider who will have no stake in the outcome.

In the first approach, the facilitator on occasion becomes involved in the discussions themselves and carries messages and proposals from one side to the other. In the second approach, the spokesperson or administrator is uninvolved in the content of discussions and acts principally as a guide to the process.

These two models are quite different, and any reader who wishes to use one or the other approach needs to understand their pros and cons. In what follows, we present two actual but disguised cases that illuminate the benefits and pitfalls of the two models and show how each works. The first case involves a long-term conflict between central engineering and plant management in a large industrial complex. The second case is a union-management conflict of long standing.

Trouble at the Elco Corporation

In this description of how the interpersonal facilitator approach worked at the Elco Corporation, we present the events chronologically through a month of negotiations.

The story & the players

The president of Elco, Stewart McFadden, had been frustrated for a long time by reports of constant bickering and poor cooperation between central engineering and plant management. Among the many things McFadden told Jim Craig when hiring him as vice president of human resources, was, "This is a nasty situation. I'd like you to take a look at it."

About a month later, when it came up again, Craig said to the president, "I've met several people from both central engineering and plant management, and it looks like quite a one-sided problem to me. The people in central engineering aren't involved that much. They feel this problem is one of those inevitable tensions in organization life, and they are trying to be patient. But the people in plant management are up in arms. They are furious."

"It's hopeless," said McFadden.

"That depends," said Craig, "on whether the problem is one of competence or of communication. If it's the former, yes, it's hopeless. If it's the latter, it's not."

"Competence? No way. They are the cream of the crop—upper 10% of graduating classes, all

of them. So it's not competence. Can you help?" McFadden asked.

"Well, I've been through a lot of hang points with unions, and in principle this situation is no different. They realize I'm a newcomer with no ax to grind. Possibly I can get them together to talk it out. At least it's worth a try."

"Anything," said McFadden. "I'm so sick of it. What do you propose?"

"I'd like to get the principals of both groups together for a day or two to get the facts out on the table. Then we'll see what can be done," said Craig.

"You've got my blessing. I look forward to whatever happens, even if you have to bang a few heads together to get their attention."

Later that week, Craig, Walt Reeves, vice president of engineering, and Jack Lewis, central coordinator of the plant management group, set up the meetings. They agreed that the purpose of the meetings was to study how the groups might cooperate. Reeves wanted Craig to take part in any negotiations as a full partner, speaking for Elco headquarters, and Lewis wanted Craig to mediate the discussions but not to formulate and present substantive proposals.

By offering the services of his office, Craig made it appropriate that he implement his own strategy. He planned for the two groups to meet initially as one large group. Craig saw himself as a facilitator. "My thought was," he reported later, "that both groups would come to know and understand each other better in a constructive atmosphere and that they would trust me to be honest and fair in my role as moderator, mediator, and, if necessary, active negotiator. I also thought that without an established agenda, the main issues would surface."

Accompanying Walt Reeves from central engineering were four of his key personnel. With Jack Lewis from the plant management group were five others—two from the plant in question and three from different plants. Craig himself was joined by other senior personnel, including the human resources advisors assigned to central engineering and to plant management. From time to time, depending on the issue, the group consulted other senior people.

Mutual trust & respect

The first meeting was held in a large room that didn't have a table. To break up a "we-they" seating arrangement and help each person participate according to his or her own convictions rather than follow a party line, Craig placed the chairs at spaced intervals around the room.

Craig, seated near the center, opened the meeting. "As you know, the president has long been concerned about how to get your groups to cooperate. He asked me to see if I could help. This meeting has no agenda beyond what the problem is and how we can solve it. Anyone is free to speak, but to keep things moving forward, I will moderate the discussion. Who'd like to start?"

"I'll tell you the problem," a member from central engineering said. "Each engineering discipline, not to mention emerging new materials and construction techniques, is becoming more complex. Plus we've got rapid changes in requirements from EPA, the Nuclear Regulatory Commission, OSHA, and half a dozen other agencies. The heavy fines for operations that violate requirements are bound to teach us all a lesson we should have learned long ago. On these scores, we've got to keep ourselves risk free. There's no option but to centralize engineering."

"That's not the problem at all," a member of plant management shot back. "We're qualified engineers, every one of us, but we are treated like children who can't be trusted to build a derrick with an erector set. It's demeaning. We manage millions in operating expenses, but we can't spend $100 on an air conditioning duct."

The meeting thereupon broke down into mutual recriminations. Later, trying a new tack, Craig stopped trying to moderate discussion between the two groups and held meetings with the two leaders instead.

From the very beginning, Craig had felt that Walt Reeves and Jack Lewis didn't trust or respect each other, and he thought that if he could get them into an informal setting, things would ease between them. He thought it was important for Reeves and Lewis to know each other better before he brought the two groups together again.

Craig wanted to accentuate the positive. He cautioned Lewis not to overreact when he first heard Reeves's formal statement about central engineering being responsible for 100% of engineering and plant management for 100% of operations.

After the first meeting between Reeves and Lewis, Craig reported that "the meeting did produce a buildup of tensions. Reeves's fixed position in regard to the 100% engineering concept was the primary reason. I already knew this to be entirely unacceptable to Lewis. We didn't make much progress, and another session was scheduled."

At this point Craig was not free to reveal to Lewis what Reeves had told him in confidence. Later Craig said, "I felt Reeves was ready to make immediate, even if minor, modifications," such as recommending an increase in the amount plant managers could authorize for small projects. Craig also knew that Reeves deeply distrusted Lewis's reasons for wanting to do "gut" engineering. He tried to help Reeves appreciate Lewis's motives.

Craig used the same strategy again and again: "When we got under way, I stepped back from the discussions because I wanted them to speak to each other directly. Soon they refrained from talking to me or even attempting to draw me into the conversation. Their talk was full of accusations and counteraccusations. Their faces became flushed. The niceties of diplomatic protocol slipped away. They had almost forgotten I was there, while I just continued taking notes.

"Eventually, the argument bogged down when each began to repeat himself and to ignore the other. By the end they were both talking at once. My attempts to change the subject were futile. As they moved toward the door, I got in front of them to block the way. I urged them not to stop these conversations but to give me another chance to use my influence. I said, 'If you have no confidence in me, then these tensions will remain.'

"Lewis agreed readily. I looked Reeves in the eye, and finally he nodded agreement. They left without speaking to each other. During the 30 or so days this effort took, I spent a lot of time preventing the sessions from being interrupted or terminated and in defending and explaining each of them to the other."

During the next few meetings, Craig took a more active role: "I began acting as a referee and made efforts to put the discussion back on track, occasionally explaining what I thought someone meant when the other person seemed to misinterpret it. After one of these sessions, when they were going back to their offices, Reeves drew me aside and said, 'Look, I don't want to talk to that SOB anymore. If you want to talk to him, you can represent my point of view, but I've had it up to here. Tell me about any progress you make, and I promise to be as constructive as possible in meeting their criticisms of us. I want you to understand the issue is not one of simply dividing engineering up in a 25-75 or a 50-50 way. Just to give them *some* will not solve the problem.'"

With this breakdown, it was no longer possible to bring the two men together to discuss their fixed positions. Craig summarized his feelings at the time this way: "I did not know where to go from there. We had accomplished little, except to name the difficult issues and to recognize the depth of disagreements. There was little or no commonality between them as men, and almost every discussion deteriorated into an unproductive argument that reopened old wounds. The final meeting ended with Reeves and Lewis casting accusations at each other."

Craig now shifted to the go-between strategy, which became the arrangement for the remainder of the month. He proposed that he be an intermediary who formulated positions. "I asked them to give me the opportunity to devise my own compromise proposals and to present my views to both of them."

As he continued to work with various individuals and subgroups within both departments, Craig drafted proposals. Then he met again with each principal to solicit reactions to his ideas. He expressed his intention to each as follows: "This proposal is drafted with the idea that neither side will alter it substantially. I've tried to keep in mind what your group wants and needs. My commitment is to continue to try to represent your interests and to negotiate for you."

Better times

The turning point in Reeves's attitude came after he and Craig had slipped into a win-lose argument about the necessity for central engineering to accept some local engineering on small-plant projects. The hot, unpleasant, and repetitive argument deteriorated until Craig stood up to leave and accused Reeves of being willing to give up peace with plant management because of an unrealistic, rigid position. Craig explained what had happened: "My strong statement made me appear tilted to the plant's perspective and therefore less trustworthy.

"In a final effort to persuade Reeves to continue these negotiations," Craig continued, "I explained the serious consequences of unilaterally breaking off. This action would harm the relationship between central engineering, the personnel function, and the corporate offices. He would be violating his promises to me, and the onus of failure would be on him. Also, I described how headquarters might give up and simply realign assignments by edict."

Reeves saw the seriousness of the situation and realized that even though he wasn't convinced about Lewis's motives or whether concessions would satisfy him, he would have to be less rigid himself.

Ultimately, the relationship between Reeves and Lewis improved, but the division of responsibility for engineering and operations did not change. Three central engineering people now provide liaison engineering. They are located so that they can quickly communicate and troubleshoot as well as provide the plant employees firsthand knowledge of in-plant engineering activities. The liaisons have reduced tensions and improved services in a variety of ways—removing bottlenecks, solving priority issues, and enabling engineering to do more realistic, functional design work. A gray area that allows plant managers to do a few functions in the name of maintenance, which in fact do involve some engineering, now exists between construction and maintenance.

What Craig did

Jim Craig's role during the negotiations shifted often. When pushed to the wall, for instance, on occasion Craig himself would become confrontational. He too became angry and fearful of disastrous consequences if something didn't change. But he kept discussion moving with many intervention techniques:

Building anticipation. Before the meetings Craig told Lewis that Reeves was coming forward with the strongest statement about a 100% to a 0% engineering-operations proposal and the reasons why. He also reported to Reeves that Lewis had no plans beyond trying to work with the situation as it developed.

Controlling discussion. When the going got tough, Craig authorized who should speak to whom and in what order, particularly in the three-way discussions: "I asked Reeves to begin—I then asked Lewis to respond—" and so forth.

Reversing antagonists' roles. Craig helped each participant clarify his understanding of the other's position by asking, "Would you repeat what Reeves just said?" and asking for confirmation: "Is that a fair statement?"

Relieving tension. After Reeves's strong initial presentation, Craig ended the strained silence by saying, "Perhaps it's appropriate now for Jack to accept the position as stated and send a memo around to that effect."

Transmitting information. Craig passed information between the two principals to prevent the process from breaking down: "I conveyed Lewis's position to Reeves by saying, 'Lewis sincerely wants to continue to explore how to make use of plant engineers to do local engineering.'"

Formulating proposals. From the beginning, Craig saw part of his job as drafting possible solutions and proposing them to the principals.

Near the end of the process, as he shuttled back and forth, Craig kept coming up with new ideas. He suggested that central engineering perform a check-and-balance function when the people in the plants did some engineering on their own. Although things do not always run smoothly at Elco, enough of the conflict has been resolved that the disagreements between engineering and plant management are not constant thorns in McFadden's side. Jim Craig continues to shuttle, keeping sparks from becoming fires.

The Hillside strike

Another, though less familiar, approach also works effectively in dealing with conflict between groups. Underlying this approach is the assumption that key leaders and their staffs in whole groups can resolve win-lose conflicts through direct confrontation.

The Hillside facility, a large modern plant serving the paper products industry, was wracked by an unresolved management-union conflict. Like true enemies, both parties had placed themselves in peril to deprive the other of a "victory."

After months of conflict, Jeff O'Hare, plant manager, said, "We are on a collision course toward a contract expiration date only months away. If a positive, productive relationship can't be established, it means another head-on clash. I'm not sure how we'd survive another shutdown as a viable economic entity, but I am sure that when and if we start up again, this plant won't be operated by the same people who are managing and operating it now."

Relationship-building strategy

Hal Floyd, corporate employee relations manager, proposed to Jeff O'Hare that they try solving their problems with the union face to face. Floyd had read about a situation similar to Hillside's in which a union and management had used the interface approach. O'Hare reluctantly agreed.

Floyd explored the possibility with the president of the local union, Rick Keenan, and then both made a joint pitch to the international union representative, Bruce Boyd. Boyd was as pessimistic and doubtful as O'Hare had been but agreed, saying, "I don't want to be accused of causing a strike because I wouldn't respond to a constructive gesture." Since no one in the company or the union could be regarded as neutral, Floyd contracted with an outsider to act as administrator.

Six members of top management and six union officials made up the two groups participating in the meetings. Because its members sat together, each group kept its feeling of solidarity. The administrator, Bob, started the sessions by reviewing goals.

"Our goal for this session is to answer the question, Can these two groups shift from a destructive relationship based on fear and suspicion to a problem-solving relationship based on respect?"

Bob explained the procedure: "As a first step, each group is to meet separately to prepare descriptions of what a sound union-management relationship would be for Hillside. You should record these on large sheets so that we can compare them at a joint session. Each group should select a spokesperson to present its conclusions in the next general session. The spokesperson may be the designated leader, but since O'Hare and Keenan have faced one another so many times in the past, it may be better to ask someone else to give your reports.

"The rest of you should try to avoid taking spontaneous potshots. They don't produce useful insights and often just cause counterattacks, which only make things worse. If you feel something important needs to be said, ask the spokesperson if you may speak. After you finish, you'll identify the similarities and differences in your separately produced descriptions to develop a consolidated model to which both groups can be committed."

He continued: "The next step is to describe the actual conditions that characterize the here and now. You'll later consolidate these into a joint statement of union-management problems at Hillside. You can then identify steps you can take to move away from the antagonistic situation to a cooperative one, with specific plans for follow-up, review, and reevaluation.

"To keep track of what's going on," he said, "I'll be in and out of both rooms, but I don't expect to take an active part. I'll be happy to answer any questions about the procedure."

Visualizing a sound relationship

At first, management seemed unable to concentrate on trying to formulate the ideal sound relationship. The session began with O'Hare questioning Keenan's, the union president's, motivations.

"I wonder what Keenan means by 'recognition'?" said O'Hare, referring to a remark Keenan had made in the joint meeting.

"Special treatment for the union president is my guess," Mike Barret, general foreman, replied. "We know they want to run the plant."

"Give 'em an inch," Allen, head of maintenance, commented supportively, "I've seen it over and over—they'll squeeze this plant dry, even dryer than it already is."

"I can't respect Keenan or his tactics," Sam Kobel, the manufacturing supervisor, said. "Maybe we'd be better off with somebody else as union president. He's a political animal. He doesn't care about the plant or the people. He just wants to move up the union ladder."

Management knew that Keenan wielded considerable influence over the membership. Wayne, the personnel manager, said, "When he person-

Exhibit I	Perceptions of actual relationship at Hillside		
	Management's view	Union's view	Consolidated view
	We have an adversary relationship. It's we versus they.	Hopelessness; a shutdown is necessary to bring them to their senses. We're ready for the shutdown.	Our adversary relationship promotes readiness for win-lose clashes; a strike is preferable to perpetual humiliation.
	There's mistrust on both sides. Cooperation means consenting to union demands. The union wants comanagement.	Cooperation is one-sided: it means doing what the company says. Hopelessness extends to all workers. Dignity is lost in a guard-prisoner relationship.	Mistrust prevails; cooperation is misinterpreted by the company as compliance and by the union as the company conceding to union demands.
	The union does not give its members a true picture of management's position. Cooperation is lacking in the promotion of efficiency and economy. Use outsiders to resolve internal issues.	Management cares only for production; people be damned. Management destroys people's incentive.	Without measuring the consequences, management concentrates on production, and the union conveys this attitude to its members.
	Management acknowledges low credibility with union members; the union president has low credibility with management.	Management blames past regimes for problems; it sees no deficiency in itself. This plant is our home for life but management's hotel until the next round of promotions.	Leaders have not earned credibility from one another; they do not make the relationship viable as a long-term investment.
	Management is only enforcing existing rules and agreement interpretation but is seen by the union as inflexible and enforcing the contract to the hilt in order to be provocative.	The union can't get its foot in the door to solve the problems.	The union accepts the exercise of initiative as a management prerogative, but management sees the union's offers of help through informal testing before decisions are finalized as comanagement.

ally favors a management proposal, he presents it at the union hall in a straightforward, positive way. If he wants a proposal rejected, he twists it to emphasize negative implications and works to see it defeated."

After venting their anger, which often participants must do before they can take a more constructive approach, management concentrated on identifying the elements of a sound relationship: mutual trust, honesty, effective communication, problem solving, and consistency. The union also started on a negative note before producing its list, which was similar to management's.

Walking toward the general session room, O'Hare overheard Melton, the shop steward, muttering to Keenan, "We'll see this kind of relationship with those buzzards when hell freezes over." Keenan nodded to the apparent truth in Melton's remark.

O'Hare shot back, "It wouldn't take long for us to agree on that, would it?" Bob, the administrator, noted this exchange but said nothing since it was not a part of the formal meetings.

When they convened in a general session to exchange their separately developed statements, the spokespersons chosen by each group made their presentations and questioned one another's meaning. The ideal relationship each proposed seemed so remote from actuality that neither the union nor management viewed it as realistic. Before sending them off to separate meeting places, Bob asked the two

groups to rate each statement in the other's report on a four-point scale:

1   "We agree with the statement as written."

2   "We agree with the statement as rewritten in the following way."

3   "We wish to ask the following questions for further clarification."

4   "We disagree with the statement for the following reasons."

He stated that each group could ask the other's spokesperson to explain the numbers and reasons for the ratings. As the two groups converted the 4's, 3's, and 2's into 1's, reflecting mutual agreement, the statements became part of the consolidated ideal model.

Getting down to brass tacks

The next step in the process is for each group to describe as objectively as possible the present reality. The members of the groups should explore specific factors that have shaped and influenced the relationship as well as the barriers that have stifled progress. At Hillside, management and the union were so preoccupied with the details of recent conflict and perceived injustice that they were anxious to begin describing actual conditions – where the real battleground was.

From management's perspective, the union was usurping authority and responsibility, thereby justifying to management its distrust and disrespect.

The union maintained that while it did not want to "run" the plant, it had much to contribute to productivity and efficiency but would withhold effort until members were treated with dignity and respect. *Exhibit I* shows how management and the union viewed the situation.

When each side revealed its view of the situation, both parties seemed stunned at the depth of the cleavage and each other's unhappiness. Recognizing that both groups had agreed to the properties of a sound relationship, management was particularly shaken by the union's conviction that, given prevailing attitudes and behavior, progress was impossible. With the plant's future on the line, along with their careers, the top managers could not reconcile themselves to giving up.

At this point each group was asked to return to its team room to digest the implications of the other's input and to apply the four-point method to the other's perception of the situation.

The tipover

The first shift in position occurred when management began comparing the two descriptions of the actual relationship, particularly the two views of "cooperation," and saw how far apart they were.

"How could two groups work in the same plant, grappling with the same problems, and see each other with such diametrically opposed viewpoints?" O'Hare asked the management group. "What do they mean, 'Cooperation is one-sided – it means doing what the company says'? During the past ten years we've given away more valuable clauses in the name of cooperation and lost more management prerogatives than any other plant in our area of competition."

"As far as I can see," said Kobel, manufacturing supervisor, "when you say 'given away,' literally that is what it's been. We've given away paragraph after paragraph and have gotten nothing in return."

"You can say that again," piped up Allen, maintenance director. "I'm so fed up with some people sitting on their fannies waiting for other people to work. If one could give a helping hand to the other, they could get the job done in half the time. We keep falling further behind."

"I propose," said Bruce Wayne, the personnel manager, "that we give this item a 4. We just flatly disagree with it."

"Hold it, fellas," said Mike Barret. "Let's look at what's been going on in the past few weeks and see how these guys could say such a thing. Any of you heard them say things in meetings you've had with them?"

"Well," said Wayne, "they think we're trying to erode the contract. They think we're putting unreasonable interpretations on various clauses and challenging them to file grievances, to which we say, 'Arbitrate.' They say this is our search-and-destroy technique."

As they continued, discussion kept returning to the first item on the union's list, "hopelessness." The contradiction between what management expected – that is, "militancy" – and what it observed – "despair and hopelessness" – compelled management to reexamine in a candid way how it could have the expectations it did.

"Does Keenan really speak for the membership when he says a strike is inevitable," O'Hare asked, "or is he just trying to shake us up?"

"It doesn't matter," Floyd said. "If he wants a strike, he can convince the people."

"And," said Mike Barret, "they know it."

"What are you hearing," questioned O'Hare, "when you talk outside the plant? Is there talk in the community about a strike? Are spouses unhappy?"

"Keenan has the strike vote in his pocket as far as I can tell," Wayne said. "He can get them riled up. If he doesn't have complete support now, he will by May. He and his cronies can convince the rest that a strike will ultimately be to their advantage. Make no mistake, he's a strong leader."

Surprised by Wayne's report of the union's reaction to what it called "unreasonable interpretations that pushed members to file grievances," O'Hare said, "Maybe we'd better look at ourselves more objectively before pointing any more fingers at them. How have you seen me relating to Keenan and the others?" he asked.

"I see you coming across as strong and hard-nosed," Allen said.

"I think you're open, forthright, and honest to the point of being naive," Floyd observed. "You've had a good reputation as a production and people man. Lately, though, I've seen you change to using force – no discussion, no alternatives, no involvement, pure force."

Wayne added, "In the past I've seen you as open, honest, fair. You listen well and take good advice. But I think you're shifting toward a tough attitude."

"I haven't seen much of a change since you've been here," Barret said. "It seems you've always been direct and aggressive."

Kobel spoke last. "I don't have much to add," he said. "Basically, I agree with what's been said. O'Hare is fair, but firm – to the point of being stubborn, I guess."

Having heard the others, O'Hare summed up his own feelings. "You're right," he said. "I think I'm so determined to turn this thing around, I've become unreasonable. It's much easier to blame our problems on my predecessors or to dump them on Keenan and his cohorts. I thought I'd kept a pretty open mind, but if my attitudes seem rigid to you, they probably seem even more so to them."

The management group then examined each member's attitude toward the union in turn. While individual differences were present, the management team shared similar attitudes, and each recognized how destructive his own actions had become. Allen ended the discussion by saying, "It's clear that we're the ones who are going to have to change."

"It won't be easy," Barret said.

"We've described the kind of relationship we want in the ideal," O'Hare said. "Now we need to decide how to get there."

"Look at what we've done in the past few months," Allen remarked. "We've created the image that we're only out for production – that we care nothing for people. They say we've destroyed the incentive for people to make any input at all."

O'Hare responded, "We don't have any choice but to try for the best relationship we can."

"I feel that's an important first step," Floyd commented. "It isn't going to be easy to turn around years of antagonism, frustration, and disappointment, and your recognition of the hard work involved is a positive sign."

"What about the rest of you?" O'Hare asked. "What do you think?"

"What other option do we have?" Kobel responded, and the others nodded affirmatively.

"What should we do now – communicate our feelings to the union?" asked Allen.

"What else is there to do?" O'Hare said.

"Okay, then, let's prepare a summary of our quandary and present it," Barret suggested.

Management made a list of five statements describing its thoughts and feelings at the time. While management grappled with its own contribution to the current conflict, the union members collected evidence of management's refusal to deal constructively.

"It's no use trying to help," they concluded. "Management sees only what it wants to, and it wants to see us as responsible for all its problems and

Exhibit II	Hillside management's description of its thoughts and feelings
1	We recognize that we have a deep win-lose orientation toward the union.
2	We want to change!
3	We have challenges to meet: to convince the union we want to change, to convince ourselves we have the patience and skill and conviction to change.
4	We're responsible for bringing the rest of management on board.
5	We recognize the risk but want to resist the temptation to revert to a win-lose stance when things get tough.

failures. What it never seems to realize is that for management Hillside is an assignment. Two, three, or four years and they're gone. For us, it's a lifetime. Do we want a plant that's not a profit maker? Nothing could be dumber. But we're not twentieth-century slaves either. We can't work overtime just to cover up their goof-offs. We can go the last mile, but to go beyond destroys our self-respect."

After each group had had the opportunity to formulate a response to the other's assessment of the actual relationship, the two groups met again to share their reactions.

Convergence of convictions

O'Hare went to Bob and said, "Look, I want to speak my own feelings, which the others agree to. Don't worry about my polarizing it."

Bob started the session by saying, "O'Hare has asked to begin by telling about management's self-study description."

O'Hare introduced the group's self-study by saying, "I guess we were concerned and angry with you in the beginning. There was a lot of blaming and finger pointing until we began really to look at ourselves." He then presented the five items shown in *Exhibit II.*

"I'd like your reactions," O'Hare said.

"Speaking for the union," Boyd, the international union representative, replied, "this comes as a total surprise, given the way things have been building up. We're really pleased that you're willing to take these steps. Both sides stand to benefit. We don't want a caucus, but we do want to go back and talk a moment among ourselves."

Leaving the room, Melton commented to Keenan, "I never believed it was possible."

O'Hare, who overheard the remark, said, "I suppose this means 'hell has frozen over'?"

"No," said Keenan, "it doesn't mean that at all."

Exhibit III   **Comparison of two approaches to intergroup problem solving**

Issue	Interpersonal facilitator model	Interface conflict-solving model
Composition	Nominal group attendance but top leaders "lead"; top leaders only	Top group plus representatives of major other constituencies who need to be involved
Contact between groups	Primarily with or through facilitator	Through spokespersons in general sessions with group integrity maintained
Facilitator or administrator to deal with	Leaders (and others) usually on a one-to-one basis	All as members of whole groups
Meetings	Exchange of entry positions	Monitoring and validation of design integrity
	Formulation of proposals and counter-proposals on a one-to-one basis by facilitator or intermediary	Ideal and actual relationship modeling on an element-by-element basis; consolidation through the four points
Communication between groups or individuals	Message-passing through facilitator	Exchanges through spokespersons, not necessarily leaders, both oral and written
	Exchange of written positions	
	Proposals made by facilitator	
Initial agenda	Perceived tensions and antagonisms	Thinking through the elements of an ideal sound relationship
Role of expert	Go-between	Procedural design administrator
	Message carrier	Not a spokesperson for other group
	Spokesperson for other group	No content role
	Solution proposer	Not a solution proposer
Tactics for dealing with an impasse	Exerting influence on members of group one to one, starting with easiest to persuade	Direct interchanges through spokespersons
	Use of acceptance and rejection to induce movement	
	Fear-provoking remarks	
Time required	Three days to one week (often longer)	Four to five days; follow-up usually months later

When the groups reconvened, Melton spoke for the union: "Our reaction is that your self-study is a giant step. We recognize it must have been hard for you to face up to the need for such drastic change. We can't tell you how welcome it is. We'll cooperate in any way to bring about the change."

Because both management and the union saw the possibility of pursuing a shared goal, each contributing from the standpoint of what was in the best interest of the plant, the tension underlying the relationship broke. This positive attitude led to a desire to get to specifics. Once the two groups gave up their antagonistic stance, they found that agreement was possible in areas where they had been deadlocked for months. For instance, at one point in the discussion of certain problems, O'Hare and Keenan were looking together at the 77 grievances that had been filed. Keenan commented, "I'm sure we've filed a number of grievances more for their annoyance value than for the merit of the issues involved."

O'Hare quickly responded, "And we've dilly-dallied in answering them and have opted for no action whenever it was legally reasonable to do so."

"We can withdraw those that have annoyance value only, identify the real issues, and clear up the situation," Keenan said.

"You won't get a no from me on that," O'Hare responded.

Smooth sailing

Several years have passed since the day O'Hare and Keenan sat down together to look at the list of grievances. How has the plant changed since the union-management meeting? In the final step of the program, ten union-management task forces grappled with problems or groups of problems. Each brought proposed solutions to the plant manager, who considered the recommendations and either approved or modified them or provided a full and satisfactory explanation for why he could not. The union has not called a strike during this time, and both union and management judge this plant to be tops in problem solving. Before the union and management got together, the plant was eleventh in the financial performance of the company's plants; today it is number one.

Bob's role

The administrator of this five-step program makes many contributions to ensure that the interface conflict-solving approach is effective. This person:

Sets expectations. Bob described the objectives and activities involved in each step of the program.

Establishes ground rules for the general sessions. Bob made sure, for instance, that up to the point where tempers quieted only the spokespersons for each group were to speak.

Determines sequence. Bob established which spokesperson would speak first. This arrangement is preferable to group members volunteering to speak first.

Monitors for candor. The design administrator monitors teams to ensure openness on a within-group basis.

Curbs open expression of hostile attitudes between groups. Bob intervened to let participants who made snide remarks know that they were breaking the ground rules.

Avoids evaluation. Bob didn't evaluate the progress or quality of group efforts, nor did he respond to inquiries regarding content or the issues being discussed.

Introduces procedures to reduce disagreements. When the group reached an impasse, Bob suggested procedures for breaking the deadlock, such as the four-point rating method.

Ensures understanding. When each spokesperson had finished speaking, Bob made sure that the other spokesperson had no further questions and that answers were to the point.

Follows up. After the meetings, Bob helped set follow-up schedules to ensure that the changes were implemented.

Which model should you use?

The interpersonal facilitator model has many adherents. The concept is inherent in the idea of the honest broker and is present when a lawyer seeks an out-of-court settlement between conflicting parties.

Exhibit IV	When to use each model

Use the interpersonal facilitator model when:	Use the interface conflict-solving model when:
Only two people are involved.	Support of group members will strengthen implementation of any change.
Personal chemistry blocks direct discussion between the principals.	Personal chemistry problems are not sufficient to prevent participation.
The leader's agreeing to change has no adverse consequences for his or her acceptability as a leader.	The leader's agreeing to change places his or her leadership in jeopardy with those who are being led.
The leaders know the depth and scope of the problem.	The leaders do not know the depth and scope of the problem.
The change can be implemented on the basis of compliance or without agreement about its soundness.	The change can best be implemented by agreement and understanding of its soundness.
A deadline is near and decisions, even though imperfect, are necessary to prevent a total breakdown.	Sufficient time is available to develop basic solutions.
A multiplicity of views exists in both groups and therefore there is no common point of view or shared feeling.	The interface problem is deeply embedded in the culture of both groups.

In each case the objective is to create a meeting of minds without dictating the terms or the outcome.

In our experience, however, the prospect of success in relieving tensions between adversary groups is much greater when managers use the interface conflict-solving approach rather than the interpersonal facilitator model. While the latter has become a more or less standard approach, it has severe limitations.

In *Exhibit III* we compare the two models in regard to some important factors such as who should comprise the groups and what the expert's role is.

Exhibit IV offers guidelines for judging which approach stands the greatest likelihood of resolving conflicts between opposing parties that impede organizational success.

The facilitator approach tends to be most successful when the outcome produced constitutes a compromise of differences and is a mutually acceptable solution to both parties, neither side feeling it has won or lost. But when membership of two or more groups is involved, that kind of compromise is hard to achieve.

Part of the power of the interface conflict-solving approach comes from the participants' lifting their thinking above the status quo to envision a model of a sound relationship. Doing so, they see the relationship in a different light and recognize the possibility of creating a new relationship rather than merely diminishing the negative aspects of the present one.

A second strength of the problem-solving approach is that it forces members of the same group to confront each other. At Hillside, Wayne challenged O'Hare to look at how management had come to use the contract as a weapon rather than as guidance for cooperation.

The reader may well ask, "Why are participants prepared to risk exposure by being open with each other, particularly when they may place themselves in jeopardy?" In many organizations, smoothly operating interfaces, say between management and the union, are crucial. When the pain it suffers from the frustration of being unable to get the job done is greater than the pain it associates with frankness, then management brings itself to the level of candor essential for focusing on the real issues.

Another compelling motivation is the rationality of problem solving. When people see something that is faulty, they want to set it right. The program of steps focuses attention on the contradictions between the sound solution and existing arrangements. When all those who feel a sense of responsibility for solving the problem see that both parties agree about what the relationship should be, they share a desire to see the problem solved.

Any executive who is involved in a conflict between groups or who is responsible for groups in dispute should seriously consider which of these two models would work in given situations. The more central and serious the issue is to the relationship between the groups, the greater the likelihood of success using the interface conflict-solving approach has. If the issue is not crucial or serious, the greater the likelihood that it can be resolved through third-party facilitation.

Beyond that, managers can always apply the facilitator model should the conflict-solving model fail, but the reverse is less likely to be true. If the facilitator approach fails, key leaders are not likely to want to try another approach, whereas if the conflict-solving model should fail, the leaders themselves may be ready to continue to seek agreement with the help of a facilitator. ▽

The indirect rewards

Conflict...is a theme that has occupied the thinking of man more than any other, save only God and love. In the vast output of discourse on the subject, conflict has been treated in every conceivable way. It has been treated descriptively, as in history and fiction; it has been treated in an aura of moral approval, as in epos; with implicit resignation, as in tragedy; with moral disapproval, as in pacifistic religions. There is a body of knowledge called military science, presumably concerned with strategies of armed conflict. There are innumerable handbooks, which teach how to play specific games of strategy. Psychoanalysts are investigating the genesis of "fight-like" situations within the individual, and social psychologists are doing the same on the level of groups and social classes....

I suspect that the most important result of a systematic and many-sided study of conflict would be the changes which such a study could effect in ourselves, the conscious and unconscious, the willing and unwilling participants in conflicts. Thus, the rewards to be realistically hoped for are the indirect ones, as was the case with the sons who were told to dig for buried treasure in the vineyard. They found no treasure, but they improved the soil.

From
Fights, Games, and Debates
by Anatol Rapoport
(Ann Arbor: University of
Michigan Press, 1960)
pp. 11, 360.
Reprinted with the permission
of the publisher.

How to run a meeting

Antony Jay

At critical points things may go wrong, but here are ways of putting them right

Why is it that any single meeting may be a waste of time, an irritant, or a barrier to the achievement of an organization's objectives? The answer lies in the fact, as the author says, that "all sorts of human crosscurrents can sweep the discussion off course, and errors of psychology and technique on the chairman's part can defeat its purposes." This article offers guidelines on how to right things that go wrong in meetings. The discussion covers the functions of a meeting, the distinctions in size and type of meetings, ways to define the objectives, making preparations, the chairman's role, and ways to conduct a meeting that will achieve its objectives.

Mr. Jay is chairman of Video Arts Ltd., a London-based producer of training films for industry. Currently, the company is producing a film (featuring John Cleese of Monty Python) on the subject of meetings, and this article springs from the research Mr. Jay did for that project. He has also written many TV documentaries, such as *Royal Family*, and authored several books, including *Management & Machiavelli* (Holt, Rinehart & Winston, 1968).

Drawings by Robert Osborn.

Why have a meeting anyway? Why indeed? A great many important matters are quite satisfactorily conducted by a single individual who consults nobody. A great many more are resolved by a letter, a memo, a phone call, or a simple conversation between two people. Sometimes five minutes spent with six people separately is more effective and productive than a half-hour meeting with them all together.

Certainly a great many meetings waste a great deal of everyone's time and seem to be held for historical rather than practical reasons; many long-established committees are little more than memorials to dead problems. It would probably save no end of managerial time if every committee had to discuss its own dissolution once a year, and put up a case if it felt it should continue for another twelve months. If this requirement did nothing else, it would at least refocus the minds of the committee members on their purposes and objectives.

But having said that, and granting that "referring the matter to a committee" can be a device for diluting authority, diffusing responsibility, and delaying decisions, I cannot deny that meetings fulfill a deep human need. Man is a social species. In every organization and every human culture of which we have record, people come together in small groups at regular and frequent intervals, and in larger "tribal" gatherings from time to time. If there are no meetings in the places where they work, people's attachment to the organizations they work for will be small, and they will meet in regular formal or

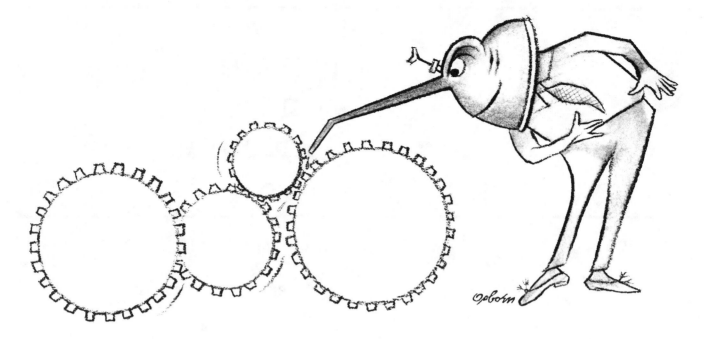

informal gatherings in associations, societies, teams, clubs, or pubs when work is over.

This need for meetings is clearly something more positive than just a legacy from our primitive hunting past. From time to time, some technomaniac or other comes up with a vision of the executive who never leaves his home, who controls his whole operation from an all-electronic, multichannel, microwave, fiber-optic video display dream console in his living room. But any manager who has ever had to make an organization work greets this vision with a smile that soon stretches into a yawn.

There is a world of science fiction, and a world of human reality; and those who live in the world of human reality know that it is held together by face-to-face meetings. A meeting still performs functions that will never be taken over by telephones, teleprinters, Xerox copiers, tape recorders, television monitors, or any other technological instruments of the information revolution.

Functions of a meeting

At this point, it may help us understand the meaning of meetings if we look at the six main functions

that meetings will always perform better than any of the more recent communication devices:

1

In the simplest and most basic way, a meeting defines the team, the group, or the unit. Those present belong to it; those absent do not. Everyone is able to look around and perceive the whole group and sense the collective identity of which he or she forms a part. We all know who we are—whether we are on the board of Universal International, in the overseas sales department of Flexitube, Inc., a member of the school management committee, on the East Hampton football team, or in Section No. 2 of Platoon 4, Company B.

2

A meeting is the place where the group revises, updates, and adds to what it knows *as a group*. Every group creates its own pool of shared knowledge, experience, judgment, and folklore. But the pool consists only of what the individuals have experienced or discussed as a group—i.e., those things which every individual knows that all the others know, too. This pool not only helps all members to do their jobs more intelligently, but it also greatly increases the speed and efficiency of all communications among them. The group knows that all special nuances and wider implications in a brief statement will be immediately clear to its members. An enormous amount of material can be left unsaid that would have to be made explicit to an outsider.

But this pool needs constant refreshing and replenishing, and occasionally the removal of impurities. So the simple business of exchanging information and ideas that members have acquired separately or in smaller groups since the last meeting is an important contribution to the strength of the group. By questioning and commenting on new contributions, the group performs an important "digestive" process that extracts what's valuable and discards the rest.

Some ethologists call this capacity to share knowledge and experience among a group "the social mind," conceiving it as a single mind dispersed among a number of skulls. They recognize that this "social mind" has a special creative power, too. A group of people meeting together can often produce better ideas, plans, and decisions than can a single individual, or a number of individuals, each working alone. The meeting can of course also produce worse outputs or none at all, if it is a bad meeting.

However, when the combined experience, knowledge, judgment, authority, and imagination of a half dozen people are brought to bear on issues, a great many plans and decisions are improved and sometimes transformed. The original idea that one person might have come up with singly is tested, amplified, refined, and shaped by argument and discussion (which often acts on people as some sort of chemical stimulant to better performance), until it satisfies far more requirements and overcomes many more objections than it could in its original form.

3
A meeting helps every individual understand both the collective aim of the group and the way in which his own and everyone else's work can contribute to the group's success.

4
A meeting creates in all present a commitment to the decisions it makes and the objectives it pursues. Once something has been decided, even if you originally argued against it, your membership in the group entails an obligation to accept the decision. The alternative is to leave the group, but in practice this is very rarely a dilemma of significance. Real opposition to decisions within organizations usually consists of one part disagreement with the decision to nine parts resentment at not being consulted before the decision. For most people on most issues, it is enough to know that their views were heard and considered. They may regret that they were not followed, but they accept the outcome.

And just as the decision of any team is binding on all the members, so the decisions of a meeting of people higher up in an organization carry a greater authority than any decision by a single executive. It is much harder to challenge a decision of the board than of the chief executive acting on his own. The decision-making authority of a meeting is of special importance for long-term policies and procedures.

5
In the world of management, a meeting is very often the only occasion where the team or group actually exists and works as a group, and the only time when the supervisor, manager, or executive is actually perceived as the leader of the team, rather than as the official to whom individuals report. In some jobs the leader does guide his team through his personal presence—not just the leader of a pit gang or construction team, but also the chef in the hotel kitchen and the maître d'hôtel in the restaurant, or the supervisor in a department store. But in large administrative headquarters, the daily or weekly meeting is often the only time when the leader is ever perceived to be guiding a team rather than doing a job.

6
A meeting is a status arena. It is no good to pretend that people are not or should not be concerned with their status relative to the other members in a group. It is just another part of human nature that we have to live with. It is a not insignificant fact that the word *order* means (a) hierarchy or pecking order; (b) an instruction or command; and (c) stability and the way things ought to be, as in "put your affairs in order," or "law and order." All three definitions are aspects of the same idea, which is indivisible.

Since a meeting is so often the only time when members get the chance to find out their relative standing, the "arena" function is inevitable. When a group is new, has a new leader, or is composed of people like department heads who are in competition for promotion and who do not work in a single team outside the meeting, "arena behavior" is likely to figure more largely, even to the point of dominating the proceedings. However, it will hardly signify with a long-established group that meets regularly.

Despite the fact that a meeting can perform all of the foregoing main functions, there is no guarantee that it will do so in any given situation. It is all too possible that any single meeting may be a waste of

time, an irritant, or a barrier to the achievement of the organization's objectives.

What sort of meeting?

While my purpose in this article is to show the critical points at which most meetings go wrong, and to indicate ways of putting them right, I must first draw some important distinctions in the size and type of meetings that we are dealing with.

Meetings can be graded by *size* into three broad categories: (1) the assembly—100 or more people who are expected to do little more than listen to the main speaker or speakers; (2) the council—40 or 50 people who are basically there to listen to the main speaker or speakers but who can come in with questions or comments and who may be asked to contribute something on their own account; and (3) the committee—up to 10 (or at the most 12) people, all of whom more or less speak on an equal footing under the guidance and control of a chairman.

We are concerned in this article only with the "committee" meeting, though it may be described as a committee, a subcommittee, a study group, a project team, a working party, a board, or by any of dozens of other titles. It is by far the most common meeting all over the world, and can perhaps be traced back to the primitive hunting band through which our species evolved. Beyond doubt it constitutes the bulk of the 11 million meetings that—so it has been calculated—take place every day in the United States.

Apart from the distinction of size, there are certain considerations regarding the *type* of meeting that profoundly affect its nature. For instance:

Frequency—A daily meeting is different from a weekly one, and a weekly meeting from a monthly one. Irregular, ad hoc, quarterly, and annual meetings are different again. On the whole, the frequency of meetings defines—or perhaps even determines—the degree of unity of the group.

Composition—Do the members work together on the same project, such as the nursing and ancillary staff on the same ward of a hospital? Do they work on different but parallel tasks, like a meeting of the company's plant managers or regional sales managers? Or are they a diverse group—strangers to each other, perhaps—united only by the meeting itself and by a common interest in realizing its objectives?

Motivation—Do the members have a common objective in their work, like a football team? Or do they to some extent have a competitive working relationship, like managers of subsidiary companies at a meeting with the chief executive, or the heads of research, production, and marketing discussing finance allocation for the coming year? Or does the desire for success through the meeting itself unify them, like a neighborhood action group or a new product design committee?

Decision process—How does the meeting group ultimately reach its decisions? By a general consensus, "the feeling of the meeting"? By a majority vote? Or are the decisions left entirely to the chairman himself, after he has listened to the facts, opinions, and discussions?

Kinds of meetings

The experienced meeting-goer will recognize that, although there seem to be five quite different methods of analyzing a meeting, in practice there is a tendency for certain kinds of meetings to sort themselves out into one of three categories. Consider:

The *daily meeting*, where people work together on the same project with a common objective and reach decisions informally by general agreement.

The *weekly* or *monthly meeting*, where members work on different but parallel projects and where there is a certain competitive element and a greater likelihood that the chairman will make the final decision himself.

The *irregular, occasional,* or *"special project"* meeting, composed of people whose normal work does not bring them into contact and whose work has little or no relationship to the others'. They are united only by the project the meeting exists to promote and motivated by the desire that the project should succeed. Though actual voting is uncommon, every member effectively has a veto.

Of these three kinds of meeting, it is the first— the workface type—that is probably the most common. It is also, oddly enough, the one most likely

to be successful. Operational imperatives usually ensure that it is brief, and the participants' experience of working side by side ensures that communication is good.

The other two types are a different matter. In these meetings all sorts of human crosscurrents can sweep the discussion off course, and errors of psychology and technique on the chairman's part can defeat its purposes. Moreover, these meetings are likely to bring together the more senior people and to produce decisions that profoundly affect the efficiency, prosperity, and even survival of the whole organization. It is, therefore, toward these higher-level meetings that the lessons of this article are primarily directed.

Before the meeting

The most important question you should ask is: "What is this meeting intended to achieve?" You can ask it in different ways—"What would be the likely consequences of not holding it?" "When it is over, how shall I judge whether it was a success or a failure?"—but unless you have a very clear requirement from the meeting, there is a grave danger that it will be a waste of everyone's time.

Defining the objective

You have already looked at the six main functions that all meetings perform, but if you are trying to use a meeting to achieve definite objectives, there are in practice only certain types of objectives it can really achieve. Every item on the agenda can be placed in one of the following four categories, or divided up into sections that fall into one or more of them:

1

Informative-digestive—Obviously, it is a waste of time for the meeting to give out purely factual information that would be better circulated in a document. But if the information should be heard from a particular person, or if it needs some clarification and comment to make sense of it, or if it has deep implications for the members of the meeting, then it is perfectly proper to introduce an item onto the agenda that requires no conclusion, decision, or action from the meeting; it is enough, simply, that the meeting should receive and discuss a report.

The "informative-digestive" function includes progress reports—to keep the group up to date on the current status of projects it is responsible for or that affect its deliberations—and review of completed projects in order to come to a collective judgment and to see what can be learned from them for the next time.

2

Constructive-originative—This "What shall we do?" function embraces all items that require something new to be devised, such as a new policy, a new strategy, a new sales target, a new product, a new marketing plan, a new procedure, and so forth. This sort of discussion asks people to contribute their knowledge, experience, judgment, and ideas. Obviously, the plan will probably be inadequate unless all relevant parties are present and pitching in.

3

Executive responsibilities—This is the "How shall we do it?" function, which comes after it has been decided what the members are going to do; at this point, executive responsibilities for the different components of the task have to be distributed around the table. Whereas in the second function the con-

tributors' importance is their knowledge and ideas, here their contribution is the responsibility for implementing the plan. The fact that they and their subordinates are affected by it makes their contribution especially significant.

It is of course possible to allocate these executive responsibilities without a meeting, by separate individual briefings, but several considerations often make a meeting desirable:

First, it enables the members as a group to find the best way of achieving the objectives.

Second, it enables each member to understand and influence the way in which his own job fits in with the jobs of the others and with the collective task.

Third, if the meeting is discussing the implementation of a decision taken at a higher level, securing the group's consent may be of prime importance. If so, the fact that the group has the opportunity to formulate the detailed action plan itself may be the decisive factor in securing its agreement, because in that case the final decision belongs, as it were, to the group. Everyone is committed to what the group decides and is collectively responsible for the final shape of the project, as well as individually answerable for his own part in it. Ideally, this sort of agenda item starts with a policy, and ends with an action plan.

4

Legislative framework: Above and around all considerations of "What to do" and "How to do it," there is a framework—a departmental or divisional organization—and a system of rules, routines, and procedures within and through which all the activity takes place. Changing this framework and introducing a new organization or new procedures can be deeply disturbing to committee members and a threat to their status and long-term security. Yet leaving it unchanged can stop the organization from adapting to a changing world. At whatever level this change happens, it must have the support of all the perceived leaders whose groups are affected by it.

The key leaders for this legislative function must collectively make or confirm the decision; if there is any important dissent, it is very dangerous to close the discussion and make the decision by decree. The group leaders cannot expect quick decisions if they are seeking to change the organization framework and routines that people have grown up with. Thus they must be prepared to leave these items unresolved for further discussion and consultation. As Francis Bacon put it—and it has never been put better—"Counsels to which time hath not been called, time will not ratify."

Making preparations

The four different functions just discussed may of course be performed by a single meeting, as the group proceeds through the agenda. Consequently, it may be a useful exercise for the chairman to go through the agenda, writing beside each item which function it is intended to fulfill. This exercise helps clarify what is expected from the discussion and helps focus on which people to bring in and what questions to ask them.

People

The value and success of a committe meeting are seriously threatened if too many people are present. Between 4 and 7 is generally ideal, 10 is tolerable, and 12 is the outside limit. So the chairman should do everything he can to keep numbers down, consistent with the need to invite everyone with an important contribution to make.

The leader may have to leave out people who expect to come or who have always come. For this job he may need tact; but since people generally preserve a fiction that they are overworked already and dislike serving on committees, it is not usually hard to secure their consent to stay away.

If the leader sees no way of getting the meeting down to a manageable size, he can try the following devices: (a) analyze the agenda to see whether everyone has to be present for every item (he may be able to structure the agenda so that some people can leave at half time and others can arrive); (b) ask himself whether he doesn't really need two separate, smaller meetings rather than one big one; and (c) determine whether one or two groups can be asked to thrash some of the topics out in advance so that only one of them needs to come in with its proposals.

Remember, too, that a few words with a member on the day before a meeting can increase the value of the meeting itself, either by ensuring that an important point is raised that comes better from the floor than from the chair or by preventing a time-wasting discussion of a subject that need not be touched on at all.

Papers

The agenda is by far the most important piece of paper. Properly drawn up, it has a power of speeding and clarifying a meeting that very few people understand or harness. The main fault is to make it unnecessarily brief and vague. For example, the phrase "development budget" tells nobody very much, whereas the longer explanation "To discuss the proposal for reduction of the 1976–1977 development budget now that the introduction of our new product has been postponed" helps all committee members to form some views or even just to look up facts and figures in advance.

Thus the leader should not be afraid of a long agenda, provided that the length is the result of his analyzing and defining each item more closely, rather than of his adding more items than the meeting can reasonably consider in the time allowed. He should try to include, very briefly, some indication of the reason for each topic to be discussed. If one item is of special interest to the group, it is often a good idea to single it out for special mention in a covering note.

The leader should also bear in mind the useful device of heading each item "For information," "For discussion," or "For decision" so that those at the meeting know where they are trying to get to.

And finally, the chairman should not circulate the agenda too far in advance, since the less organized members will forget it or lose it. Two or three days is about right—unless the supporting papers are voluminous.

Other 'paper' considerations: The order of items on the agenda is important. Some aspects are obvious—the items that need urgent decision have to come before those that can wait till next time. Equally, the leader does not discuss the budget for the reequipment program before discussing whether to put the reequipment off until next year. But some aspects are not so obvious. Consider:

□

The early part of a meeting tends to be more lively and creative than the end of it, so if an item needs mental energy, bright ideas, and clear heads, it may be better to put it high up on the list. Equally, if there is one item of great interest and concern to everyone, it may be a good idea to hold it back for a while and get some other useful work done first. Then the star item can be introduced to carry the meeting over the attention lag that sets in after the first 15 to 20 minutes of the meeting.

□

Some items unite the meeting in a common front while others divide the members one from another. The leader may want to start with unity before entering into division, or he may prefer the other way around. The point is to be aware of the choice and to make it consciously, because it is apt to make a difference to the whole atmosphere of the meeting. It is almost always a good idea to find a unifying item with which to end the meeting.

□

A common fault is to dwell too long on trivial but urgent items, to the exclusion of subjects of fundamental importance whose significance is long-term rather than immediate. This can be remedied by putting on the agenda the time at which discussion of the important long-term issue will begin—and by sticking to it.

□

Very few business meetings achieve anything of value after two hours, and an hour and a half is enough time to allocate for most purposes.

□

It is often a good idea to put the finishing time of a meeting on the agenda as well as the starting time.

□

If meetings have a tendency to go on too long, the chairman should arrange to start them one hour before lunch or one hour before the end of work. Generally, items that ought to be kept brief can be introduced ten minutes from a fixed end point.

□

The practice of circulating background or proposal papers along with the minutes is, in principle, a good one. It not only saves time, but it also helps in formulating useful questions and considerations in advance. But the whole idea is sabotaged once the papers get too long; they should be brief or provide a short summary. If they are circulated, obviously the chairman has to read them, or at least must not be caught not having read them.

(One chairman, more noted for his cunning than his conscientiousness, is said to have spent 30 seconds before each meeting going through all the papers he had not read with a thick red pen, marking lines and question marks in the margins at random, and making sure these were accidentally made visible to the meeting while the subject was being discussed.)

□

If papers are produced at the meeting for discussion, they should obviously be brief and simple, since everyone has to read them. It is a supreme folly to bring a group of people together to read six pages of closely printed sheets to themselves. The exception is certain kinds of financial and statistical papers whose function is to support and illustrate verbal points as reference documents rather than to be swallowed whole: these are often better tabled at the meeting.

□

All items should be thought of and thought about in advance if they are to be usefully discussed. Listing "Any other business" on the agenda is an invitation to waste time. This does not absolutely preclude the chairman's announcing an extra agenda item at a meeting if something really urgent and unforeseen crops up or is suggested to him by a member, provided it is fairly simple and straightforward. Nor does it preclude his leaving time for general unstructured discussion after the close of the meeting.

□

The chairman, in going through the agenda items in advance, can usefully insert his own brief notes of points he wants to be sure are not omitted from the discussion. A brief marginal scribble of "How much notice?" or "Standby arrangements?" or whatever is all that is necessary.

The chairman's job

Let's say that you have just been appointed chairman of the committee. You tell everyone that it is a bore or a chore. You also tell them that you have been appointed "for my sins." But the point is that you tell them. There is no getting away from it: some sort of honor or glory attaches to the chairman's role. Almost everyone is in some way pleased and proud to be made chairman of something. And that is three quarters of the trouble.

Master or servant?

Their appointment as committee chairman takes people in different ways. Some seize the opportunity to impose their will on a group that they see themselves licensed to dominate. Their chairmanship is a harangue, interspersed with demands for group agreement.

Others are more like scoutmasters, for whom the collective activity of the group is satisfaction enough, with no need for achievement. Their chairmanship is more like the endless stoking and fueling of a campfire that is not cooking anything.

And there are the insecure or lazy chairmen who look to the meeting for reassurance and support in their ineffectiveness and inactivity, so that they can spread the responsibility for their indecisiveness among the whole group. They seize on every expression of disagreement or doubt as a justification for avoiding decision or action.

But even the large majority who do not go to those extremes still feel a certain pleasurable tumescence of the ego when they take their place at the head of the table for the first time. The feeling is no sin: the sin is to indulge it or to assume that the pleasure is shared by the other members of the meeting.

It is the chairman's self-indulgence that is the greatest single barrier to the success of a meeting. His first duty, then, is to be aware of the temptation and of the dangers of yielding to it. The clearest of the danger signals is hearing himself talking a lot during a discussion.

One of the best chairmen I have ever served under makes it a rule to restrict her interventions to a single sentence, or at most two. She forbids herself ever to contribute a paragraph to a meeting she is chairing. It is a harsh rule, but you would be hard put to find a regular attender of her meetings (or anyone else's) who thought it was a bad one.

There is, in fact, only one legitimate source of pleasure in chairmanship, and that is pleasure in the achievements of the meeting—and to be legitimate, it must be shared by all those present. Meetings are *necessary* for all sorts of basic and primitive human reasons, but they are *useful* only if they are seen by all present to be getting somewhere—and somewhere they know they could not have gotten to individually.

If the chairman is to make sure that the meeting achieves valuable objectives, he will be more effective seeing himself as the servant of the group rather than as its master. His role then becomes that of assisting the group toward the best conclusion or decision in the most efficient manner possible: to interpret and clarify; to move the discussion forward; and to bring it to a resolution that everyone understands and accepts as being the will of the meeting, even if the individuals do not necessarily agree with it.

His true source of authority with the members is the strength of his perceived commitment to their combined objective and his skill and efficiency in helping and guiding them to its achievement. Control and discipline then become not the act of imposing his will on the group but of imposing the group's will on any individual who is in danger of diverting or delaying the progress of the discussion and so from realizing the objective.

Once the members realize that the leader is impelled by his commitment to their common objective, it does not take great force of personality for him to control the meeting. Indeed, a sense of urgency and a clear desire to reach the best conclusion as quickly as possible are a much more effective disciplinary instrument than a big gavel. The effective chairman can then hold the discussion to the point by indicating that there is no time to pursue a particular idea now, that there is no time for long speeches, that the group has to get through

this item and on to the next one, rather than by resorting to pulling rank.

There are many polite ways the chairman can indicate a slight impatience even when someone else is speaking—by leaning forward, fixing his eyes on the speaker, tensing his muscles, raising his eyebrows, or nodding briefly to show the point is taken. And when replying or commenting, the chairman can indicate by the speed, brevity, and finality of his intonation that "we have to move on." Conversely, he can reward the sort of contribution he is seeking by the opposite expressions and intonations, showing that there is plenty of time for that sort of idea, and encouraging the speaker to develop the point.

After a few meetings, all present readily understand this nonverbal language of chairmanship. It is the chairman's chief instrument of educating the group into the general type of "meeting behavior" that he is looking for. He is still the servant of the group, but like a hired mountain guide, he is the one who knows the destination, the route, the weather signs, and the time the journey will take. So if he suggests that the members walk a bit faster, they take his advice.

This role of servant rather than master is often obscured in large organizations by the fact that the chairman is frequently the line manager of the members: this does not, however, change the reality of the role of chairman. The point is easier to see in, say, a neighborhood action group. The question in that case is, simply, "Through which person's chairmanship do we collectively have the best chance of getting the children's playground built?"

However, one special problem is posed by this definition of the chairman's role, and it has an extremely interesting answer. The question is: How can the chairman combine his role with the role of a member advocating one side of an argument?

The answer comes from some interesting studies by researchers who sat in on hundreds of meetings to find out how they work. Their consensus finding is that most of the effective discussions have, in fact, two leaders: one they call a "team," or "social," leader; the other a "task," or "project," leader.

Regardless of whether leadership is in fact a single or a dual function, for our purposes it is enough to say that the chairman's best role is that of social leader. If he wants a particular point to be strongly advocated, he ensures that it is someone else who leads off the task discussion, and he holds back until much later in the argument. He might indeed change or modify his view through hearing the discussion, but even if he does not it is much easier for him to show support for someone else's point later in the discussion, after listening to the arguments. Then, he can summarize in favor of the one he prefers.

The task advocate might regularly be the chairman's second-in-command, or a different person might advocate for different items on the agenda. On some subjects, the chairman might well be the task advocate himself, especially if they do not involve conflict within the group. The important point is that the chairman has to keep his "social leadership" even if it means sacrificing his "task leadership." However, if the designated task advocate persists in championing a cause through two or three meetings, he risks building up quite a head of antagonism to him among the other members. Even so, this antagonism harms the group less by being directed at the "task leader" than at the "social leader."

Structure of discussion

It may seem that there is no right way or wrong way to structure a committee meeting discussion.

A subject is raised, people say what they think, and finally a decision is reached, or the discussion is terminated. There is some truth in this. Moreover, it would be a mistake to try and tie every discussion of every item down to a single immutable format.

Nevertheless, there is a logical order to a group discussion, and while there can be reasons for not following it, there is no justification for not being aware of it. In practice, very few discussions are inhibited, and many are expedited, by a conscious adherence to the following stages, which follow exactly the same pattern as a visit to the doctor:

"What seems to be the trouble?" The reason for an item being on a meeting agenda is usually like the symptom we go to the doctor with: "I keep getting this pain in my back" is analogous to "Sales have risen in Germany but fallen in France." In both cases it is clear that something is wrong and that something ought to be done to put it right. But until the visit to the doctor, or the meeting of the European marketing committee, that is about all we really know.

"How long has this been going on?" The doctor will start with a case history of all the relevant background facts, and so will the committee discussion. A solid basis of shared and agreed-on facts is the best foundation to build any decision on, and a set of pertinent questions will help establish it. For example, when did French sales start to fall off? Have German sales risen exceptionally? Has France had delivery problems, or less sales effort, or weaker advertising? Have we lost market share, or are our competitors' sales falling too? If the answers to all these questions, and more, are not established at the start, a lot of discussion may be wasted later.

"Would you just lie down on the couch?" The doctor will then conduct a physical examination to find out how the patient is now. The committee, too, will want to know how things stand at this moment. Is action being taken? Do long-term orders show the same trend? What are the latest figures? What is the current stock position? How much money is left in the advertising budget?

"You seem to have slipped a disc." When the facts are established, you can move toward a dignosis. A doctor may seem to do this quickly, but that is the result of experience and practice. He is, in fact, rapidly eliminating all the impossible or far-fetched explanations until he leaves himself with a short list. The committee, too, will hazard and eliminate a

variety of diagnoses until it homes in on the most probable—for example, the company's recent energetic and highly successful advertising campaign in Germany plus new packaging by the market leader in France.

"Take this round to the druggist." Again, the doctor is likely to take a shortcut that a committee meeting may be wise to avoid. The doctor comes out with a single prescription, and the committee, too, may agree quickly on a single course of action.

But if the course is not so clear, it is better to take this step in two stages: (a) construct a series of options—do not, at first, reject any suggestions outright but try to select and combine the promising elements from all of them until a number of thought-out, coherent, and sensible suggestions are on the table; and (b) only when you have generated these options do you start to choose among them. Then you can discuss and decide whether to pick the course based on repackaging and point-of-sale promotion, or the one based on advertising and a price cut, or the one that bides its time and saves the money for heavier new-product promotion next year.

If the item is at all complex or especially significant, it is important for the chairman not only to have the proposed course of the discussion in his own head, but also to announce it so that everyone knows. A good idea is to write the headings on an easel pad with a felt pen. This saves much of the time wasting and confusion that result when people raise items in the wrong place because they were not privy to the chairman's secret that the right place was coming up later on in the discussion.

Conducting the meeting

Just as the driver of a car has two tasks, to follow his route and to manage his vehicle, so the chairman's job can be divided into two corresponding tasks, dealing with the subject and dealing with the people.

Dealing with the subject

The essence of this task is to follow the structure of discussion as just described in the previous section. This, in turn, entails listening carefully and keeping the meeting pointed toward the objective.

At the start of the discussion of any item, the chairman should make it clear where the meeting should try to get to by the end. Are the members hoping to make a clear decision or firm recommendation? Is it a preliminary deliberation to give the members something to go away with and think about? Are they looking for a variety of different lines to be pursued outside the meeting? Do they have to approve the proposal, or merely note it?

The chairman may give them a choice: "If we can agree on a course of action, that's fine. If not, we'll have to set up a working party to report and recommend before next month's meeting."

The chairman should make sure that all the members understand the issue and why they are discussing it. Often it will be obvious, or else they may have been through it before. If not, then he or someone he has briefed before the meeting should give a short introduction, with some indication of the reason the item is on the agenda; the story so far; the present position; what needs to be established, resolved, or proposed; and some indication of lines of inquiry or courses of action that have been suggested or explored, as well as arguments on both sides of the issue.

If the discussion is at all likely to be long or complex, the chairman should propose to the meeting a structure for it with headings (written up if necessary), as I stated at the end of the section on "Structure of discussion." He should listen carefully in case people jump too far ahead (e.g., start proposing a course of action before the meeting has agreed on the cause of the trouble), or go back over old ground, or start repeating points that have been made earlier. He has to head discussion off sterile or irrelevant areas very quickly (e.g., the rights and wrongs of past decisions that it is too late to change, or distant prospects that are too remote to affect present actions).

It is the chairman's responsibility to prevent misunderstanding and confusion. If he does not follow an argument or understand a reference, he should seek clarification from the speaker. If he thinks two people are using the same word with different meanings, he should intervene (e.g., one member using *promotion* to mean point-of-sale advertising only, and another also including media publicity).

He may also have to clarify by asking people for facts or experience that perhaps influence their view but are not known to others in the meeting. And he should be on the lookout for points where an interim summary would be helpful. This device frequently takes only a few seconds, and acts like a life belt to some of the members who are getting out of their depth.

Sometimes a meeting will have to discuss a draft document. If there are faults in it, the members should agree on what the faults are and the chairman should delegate someone to produce a new draft later. The group should never try to redraft around the table.

Perhaps one of the most common faults of chairmanship is the failure to terminate the discussion early enough. Sometimes chairmen do not realize that the meeting has effectively reached an agreement, and consequently they let the discussion go on for another few minutes, getting nowhere at all. Even more often, they are not quick enough to close a discussion *before* agreement has been reached.

A discussion should be closed once it has become clear that (a) more facts are required before further progress can be made, (b) discussion has revealed that the meeting needs the views of people not present, (c) members need more time to think about the subject and perhaps discuss it with colleagues, (d) events are changing and likely to alter or clarify the basis of the decision quite soon, (e) there is not going to be enough time at this meeting to go over the subject properly, or (f) it is becoming clear that two or three of the members can settle this outside the meeting without taking up the time of the rest. The fact that the decision is difficult, likely to be disputed, or going to be unwelcome to somebody, however, is not a reason for postponement.

At the end of the discussion of each agenda item, the chairman should give a brief and clear summary of what has been agreed on. This can act as the dictation of the actual minutes. It serves not merely to put the item on record, but also to help people realize that something worthwhile has been achieved. It also answers the question "Where did all that get us?" If the summary involves action by a member of the meeting, he should be asked to confirm his acceptance of the undertaking.

Dealing with the people

There is only one way to ensure that a meeting starts on time, and that is to start it on time. Latecomers who find that the meeting has begun without them soon learn the lesson. The alternative is that the prompt and punctual members will soon realize that a meeting never starts until ten minutes after the advertised time, and they will also learn the lesson.

Punctuality at future meetings can be wonderfully reinforced by the practice of listing late arrivals (and early departures) in the minutes. Its ostensible and perfectly proper purpose is to call the latecomer's attention to the fact that he was absent when a decision was reached. Its side effect, however, is to tell everyone on the circulation list that he was late, and people do not want that sort of information about themselves published too frequently.

There is a growing volume of work on the significance of seating positions and their effect on group behavior and relationships. Not all the findings are generally agreed on. What does seem true is that:

□
Having members sit face to face across a table facilitates opposition, conflict, and disagreement, though of course it does not turn allies into enemies. But

it does suggest that the chairman should think about whom he seats opposite himself.

□

Sitting side by side makes disagreements and confrontation harder. This in turn suggests that the chairman can exploit the friendship-value of the seats next to him.

□

There is a "dead man's corner" on the chairman's right, especially if a number of people are seated in line along from him (it does not apply if he is alone at the head of the table).

□

As a general rule, proximity to the chairman is a sign of honor and favor. This is most marked when he is at the head of a long, narrow table. The greater the distance, the lower the rank—just as the lower-status positions were "below the salt" at medieval refectories.

Control the garrulous

In most meetings someone takes a long time to say very little. As chairman, your sense of urgency should help indicate to him the need for brevity. You can also suggest that if he is going to take a long time it might be better for him to write a paper. If it is urgent to stop him in full flight, there is a useful device of picking on a phrase (it really doesn't matter what phrase) as he utters it as an excuse for cutting in and offering it to someone else: "Inevitable decline—that's very interesting. George, do you agree that the decline is inevitable?"

Draw out the silent

In any properly run meeting, as simple arithmetic will show, most of the people will be silent most of the time. Silence can indicate general agreement, or no important contribution to make, or the need to wait and hear more before saying anything, or too good a lunch, and none of these need worry you. But there are two kinds of silence you must break:

1

The silence of diffidence. Someone may have a valuable contribution to make but be sufficiently nervous about its possible reception to keep it to himself. It is important that when you draw out such a contribution, you should express interest and pleasure (though not necessarily agreement) to encourage further contributions of that sort.

2

The silence of hostility. This is not hostility to ideas, but to you as the chairman, to the meeting, and to the process by which decisions are being reached.

This sort of total detachment from the whole proceedings is usually the symptom of some feeling of affront. If you probe it, you will usually find that there is something bursting to come out, and that it is better out than in.

Protect the weak

Junior members of the meeting may provoke the disagreement of their seniors, which is perfectly reasonable. But if the disagreement escalates to the point of suggesting that they have no right to contribute, the meeting is weakened. So you may have to take pains to commend their contribution for its usefulness, as a pre-emptive measure. You can reinforce this action by taking a written note of a point they make (always a plus for a member of a meeting) and by referring to it again later in the discussion (a double-plus).

Encourage the clash of ideas

But, at the same time, discourage the clash of personalities. A good meeting is not a series of dialogues between individual members and the chairman. Instead, it is a crossflow of discussion and debate, with the chairman occasionally guiding, mediating, probing, stimulating, and summarizing, but mostly letting the others thrash ideas out. However, the meeting must be a contention of *ideas*, not people.

If two people are starting to get heated, widen the discussion by asking a question of a neutral member of the meeting, preferably a question that requires a purely factual answer.

Watch out for the suggestion-squashing reflex

Students of meetings have reduced everything that can be said into questions, answers, positive reactions, and negative reactions. Questions can only seek, and answers only supply, three types of response: information, opinion, and suggestion.

In almost every modern organization, it is the suggestions that contain the seeds of future success. Although very few suggestions will ever lead to anything, almost all of them need to be given every chance. The trouble is that suggestions are much easier to ridicule than facts or opinions. If people feel that making a suggestion will provoke the negative reaction of being laughed at or squashed, they will soon stop. And if there is any status-jostling going on at the meeting, it is all too easy to use the occasion of someone's making a suggestion as the opportunity to take him down a peg. It is all too easy and a formula to ensure sterile meetings.

The answer is for you to take special notice and show special warmth when anyone makes a suggestion, and to discourage as sharply as you can the squashing-reflex. This can often be achieved by requiring the squasher to produce a better suggestion on the spot. Few suggestions can stand up to squashing in their pristine state: your reflex must be to pick out the best part of one and get the other committee members to help build it into something that might work.

Come to the most senior people last
Obviously, this cannot be a rule, but once someone of high authority has pronounced on a topic, the less senior members are likely to be inhibited. If you work up the pecking order instead of down it, you are apt to get a wider spread of views and ideas. But the juniors who start it off should only be asked for contributions within their personal experience and competence. ("Peter, you were at the Frankfurt Exhibition—what reactions did you pick up there?")

Close on a note of achievement
Even if the final item is left unresolved, you can refer to an earlier item that was well resolved as you close the meeting and thank the group.

If the meeting is not a regular one, fix the time and place of the next one before dispersing. A little time spent with appointment diaries at the end, especially if it is a gathering of five or more members, can save hours of secretarial telephoning later.

Following the meeting

Your secretary may take the minutes (or better still, one of the members), but the minutes are your responsibility. They can be very brief, but they should include these facts:

☐
The time and date of the meeting, where it was held, and who chaired it.
☐
Names of all present and apologies for absence.
☐
All agenda items (and other items) discussed and all decisions reached. If action was agreed on, record (and underline) the name of the person responsible for the assignment.
☐
The time at which the meeting ended (important, because it may be significant later to know whether the discussion lasted 15 minutes or 6 hours).
☐
The date, time, and place of the next committee meeting.

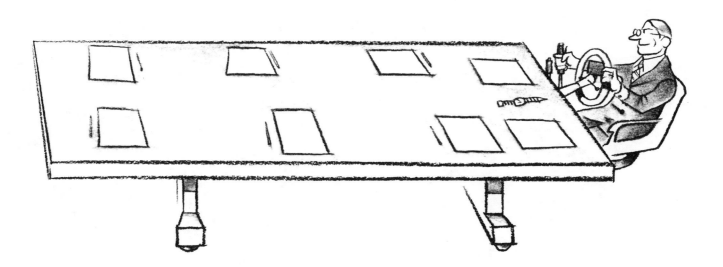

Meetings That Work: Plans Bosses Can Approve

Design your plan to answer four key questions.

by Paul D. Lovett

With his business under severe pressure, a group vice president went into his annual strategic-plan meeting with top management carrying nothing more than a large, pencil-draft spread sheet. He brought along no plan document, no overhead slides, and none of his operating staff. But using that simple spread sheet, he identified the difficult options facing his ailing subsidiary and presented his plan. The company's top half-dozen executives hotly debated the proposal, peppering him with questions. Finally, the chairman overruled his aides and opted to continue to invest in the business.

Of the many meetings I attended as manager of corporate planning for a $2 billion industrial gas products company, that one taught me the most about how planning decisions are made—and not made—in a large corporation.

Clearly, there is a substantial gap between planning theory and its practice. Planning meetings are typified by players concerned mostly

with covering their own rear ends—too busy putting out fires to think about the future and afraid to nail down a decision that would mean ac-

> █ The meeting is where the plan becomes real—where the decision is up or down.

countability. Decision makers are as often motivated by friendships, concerns for popularity, and self-interest as by the cold, hard facts gleaned from rigorous analysis. Planning documents too often ignore what's really at stake among participants and fail to establish a logical, agreed-on course of action.

My first task as manager of planning, in fact, was to redesign the bulky forms the company used in its

annual planning exercise. At that time, the company generated plan *books*, and by the end of the planning cycle, the president would have a foot-high stack of these thick, three-ring binders crammed with facts, figures, charts, and endless prose about markets and competitors. The problem was, top decision makers didn't read the plan books because they weren't helpful as a guide for action.

I soon discovered that it wasn't just the plan books that didn't work. Almost nothing formally written down or presented worked. Strategic plans were not read, presentations seldom inspired a creative exchange of ideas, portfolio analysis was disregarded, and financial forecasts had no credibility. Managers were only going through the planning process because corporate had asked them to fill in some forms or make a presentation. They saw no value in it for themselves.

The document-oriented planning process did not take into account that key executives spend much of their time in meetings, not writing long documents or reading them, and the more senior the position, the more exaggerated this phenomenon becomes.

The VP of that crisis-ridden subsidiary understood the hidden agendas and preoccupations of his superiors when he reduced his proposal to its essentials. The simple lesson he taught me was that the meeting is where the plan becomes real—where the decision up or down is made. If you want your bosses to approve your idea, you have to sell them on it. You first must get them to focus on the elements you deem important—your vision and your plan of action. And that requires simplicity. Nobody is going to focus on a dull recitation of turgid mush. They certainly won't remember it, and if people can't remember what was

Paul D. Lovett, president of P.D. Lovett & Company in Allentown, Pennsylvania, is a management consultant focusing on business planning. His 20 years' experience includes a variety of line-management and business-planning positions for private industry and government.

said at the meeting, then no planning got done.

This article, then, is really about meetings more than plans, meetings where a decision is sought from the boss – approval of a capital budget, the purchase of a piece of equipment, an increase in the work force.

Over the years I have come to realize that chief executive officers want four questions answered before they will approve a plan:

1. What is the plan?
2. Why is the plan recommended?
3. What are the goals?
4. How much will it cost to implement the plan?

If you satisfactorily answer these questions for the decision maker, chances are you'll get your decision.

You should limit the written presentation of each of the four points to one page. It may be tough to summarize the programs for a $500 million business on a single sheet of paper, but I've found it is usually possible. Moreover, it will make *you* focus on what you want and why you want it.

This four-part approach to planning is straightforward enough, but the real planning must occur *before* the meeting when you and your staff shape the agenda and package the information to make your case convincing. It is at these earlier meetings, too, that you and your staff accept responsibility for the plan and for making it a reality. And you can use these meetings not only for planning but also for building your network of supporters.

A divisional manager of a $40 million specialty business used the four-step process to develop his plan, and at each preparatory meeting he included the managers from R&D, manufacturing, sales, and marketing. By the time the plan was finally presented to his boss, each member of the task force felt a part of the team and was already prepared to implement the plan. The preparation had created the impetus for approval and for execution once approval was given.

What is the plan?

Answering this question requires a positive and specific future-tense statement of strategy that the CEO can accept or reject: "The auto products division will acquire a chain of muffler shops." Then you list the actions that will support the plan, like studying the kinds of acquisitions sought and the market areas and hiring an investment banker to help pursue the right deals. Programs at

> ## The real planning occurs *before* the meeting, when you shape the agenda.

this level might lay the groundwork for a series of capital expenditures that you will request the following year. They might propose a major reorganization, establish a pricing policy, or target a market segment. The statement and list are enough to get the discussion started.

While all this may seem basic enough, I have found that many presentations don't discuss the plan itself. They'll forecast performance and describe environments, but they won't sketch out the action to be taken.

Sometimes, to avoid confrontation, presenters use general statements that may sound like a strategy. "Margins will be increased by focusing on the high-growth segments of the market" is one often-used statement. Now who would deny the wisdom of that approach? If you think about it, it's a good approach for the other business units in the division or for the whole company, in fact for nearly all units in every company, everywhere. It's not a strategy, however. It's not specific enough to provide guidance for anything. How will the unit raise its margins, by how much, and in what time frame? What are the high-growth segments of the market?

Often, business managers won't volunteer answers to such questions. Why should they take the risk, after all? It's tough to call the future, and they'd rather wait to see how things turn out. But by then, of course, it will be too late to imple-

ment an effective strategy for taking advantage of the situation.

The following statement, still very short, provides far greater insight into the intentions of the business unit: "The sales staff will be doubled so we can expand into the New York–New Jersey electronics market." Now there is something to discuss with the president. The high-potential market segment is identified, and the means and magnitude of the proposed solution are outlined.

To be effective, those who report directly to the decision maker must establish *their* plan – not one that is simply a conglomeration of subordinate-unit plans but one that establishes priorities among those units. At the industrial gas company, the group VPs who reported to the president were seldom central participants in the process. Most saw it as an opportunity to parade their staff in front of senior management. The group VP assumed the role of the reviewing party rather than the party under review. Consequently, the president was not getting the group VP's plan but what could be more aptly described as a laundry list of items that the business managers wanted to accomplish. After the meetings, the operating execs would frequently complain about the president meddling with the details of their business. But how could he do otherwise until they stopped delivering the details and started presenting a strategically oriented message?

Why is the plan recommended?

The definitive programs, once established, will be successful only as long as the boss remains confident that the opportunity is attractive and that there is a basis for competitive advantage. It is crucial, therefore, to make the plan's rationale clear to the decision maker. You're laying out what the situation is.

Even fail-safe ideas need to be thoroughly supported. One VP went into a plan meeting with the president and asked for permission to open an office in Southeast Asia. To the VP, the need for the company's presence on the Pacific Rim was obvious, and the cost was so low – only

"This is what comes of making it into top executive rank?—an obscene conference call!"

$1 million—that he thought approval was in the bag. But he hadn't studied the market or hypothesized a rate of return, so he couldn't demonstrate the value of the investment. The president told him no. "But it's only $1 million," the surprised vice president said. "A million dollars is a lot of money, even for us," the president responded.

Operating managers rarely face the CEO to discuss planning issues and may think they need to brief him or her on every last fact about the market and the situation. This only results in the rationale getting muddled, either by too much detail or by a failure to delve into real operations issues. Remember, CEOs don't have the time to address the details of any one subject. It's up to the manager, therefore, to synthesize the rationale in such a way as to give the CEO confidence in the information and conclusions. And that requires thorough research—of the markets, competition, costs, and whatever else is important to the logic of the proposal. You've got to know the environment in which your programs will be operating.

To control the tendency toward overkill, some companies insist managers draw up a list of key issues that will help establish the rationale for a plan. This part of the process can generate a high level of interest. But even here, the temptation is to discuss the issues so thoroughly that no time is left to decide what to do about them, what programs to create.

The more prevalent problem is that the boss doesn't get *enough* synthesized information. People want to know what the boss thinks before they play their cards. In effect, they want the CEO to tell them what the solution is instead of the other way around. It thus seems much easier to state the concern as a question: "What are we going to do about the fluctuating price of oil? Will a new competitor enter the market? What will be the rate of growth of the product?"

The implication is that any actions the manager will propose depend on the results of the question. Frequently, in fact, the stated issues are about things over which the unit manager has no control (take a sec-

ond look at the questions above). Presenters highlight the price of oil or the economy as an issue because they know there is no correct solution against which they can later be evaluated.

Managers may also try to avoid confronting senior management with real issues and definitive programs. Here is an example. At each annual planning meeting, the VP of the international division would discuss budgets and projections of all his units, including the one in South Africa. Despite public pressure on U.S. companies with operations there, the VP would not focus on the question, "Should we maintain our position in South Africa or change it?" As a consequence, the key executives deferred debate on an exit strategy, leaving little time to evaluate the costs and benefits of getting out or looking at prospective buyers. Two years later, the unit was sold, but from a far more disadvantageous bargaining position.

All meeting participants bear a certain responsibility. If the meeting is to be useful, everyone needs to view the proposal as something to be negotiated and agreed on. Gaining consensus on the presenter's outline of programs is the primary objective of the entire planning exercise. Without consensus there is no plan.

Managers will get good feedback only if they propose specific programs that map out well-defined

Overfocusing on numbers may obscure market realities.

courses of action. Both presenter and staff should be able to proceed from the meeting with the confidence that senior management will be supportive. When strategies and programs are not specific, managers will have to qualify anew each individual initiative as it arises in succeeding months—negating the intended purpose of the planning exercise.

For their part, when executives have doubts, they have the responsibility to question their subordinates' conclusions. Unless the doubts are aired, there will be no shared commitment to the plan, and it will be doomed to failure – either because the doubts were valid or because in the long run the boss simply will not support the tactical programs necessary to carry out the plan.

Executives must also feel responsible for accepting or rejecting the various parts of the proposal, rather than just reviewing them – or interjecting their own off-the-cuff proposal, such as what happened at one top-level plan meeting.

Near the end, the president mentioned two new industries that had not been discussed but that he believed should get marketing attention. Even though nobody had investigated those industries, the group VP's concluding remark was, "Okay, we will give attention to those markets but let's remember what we said when budget time comes." His implication was that people or monetary resources would be applied to the new industries. Yet he and the president had not agreed on goals or a level of expenditure for the program. Consequently, nothing was done. Even the president's program had to wait until it had more definition.

What are the goals?

The goals are what you expect to happen if the plan is adopted. A planning system requiring managers to identify and defend specific goals yields more realistic forecasts because managers realize their success can be carefully monitored. While this makes the plan presenter less comfortable, it gives senior management better control over the operation.

It is possible, in fact necessary, to limit the financial detail to a few important numbers. First, get the conversation focused on the unit of measure, not the numerical values. Is the business manager's objective to increase earnings or to gain an improved share position? A simple chart can then illustrate what the goals are and how they compare with the present situation. In some special cases, a list of milestones may

summarize the goal better than a numerical target.

Just a few numbers are enough to focus the goals discussion on the right issues. For example, how is the business doing today in terms of share position, sales, and earnings, and how do we expect to be doing five years from now in each of these categories?

Often, though, when executives speak of their goals, they are mis-

> Controllers struggle over next year's budget; how can they project five years out?

takenly thinking about just their financial forecasts. A unit manager, therefore, will push responsibility for developing the plan onto the controller. The manager may hold a perfunctory meeting to establish a sales scenario, and then will shuffle onto the controller the burden of working up the details and perhaps even presenting the plan. Controllers invest significant time and effort into forecasting sales, detailing costs, and projecting net incomes. So the numbers become the principal output of the plan.

There is one problem: the numbers are frequently worthless. Controllers struggle to get next year's budget close; they cannot be expected to project reasonable numbers five years out. Moreover, business managers typically want the numbers to show increased share, the introduction of new products, and increased profitability all at the same time. The industrial gas company's 1980 plan, which was based on all the units' projections, reflects what often happens. Sales would reach $3 billion in five years and profits, $246 million, the plan said. The results were not even close. Sales in 1985, a good year, were $1.8 billion; earnings were $143 million. A year later, a major write-down left earnings at only $5 million.

The numbers, then, are only a part of the proposal, and by overfocusing on them, a unit is prone to overlook market realities. The industrial gas company, for example, holding a highly profitable leadership position in the U.S. market for hydrogen, foresaw an opportunity to enter the European market. At the time, there was no commercial distributor of the product in Europe. The company had a choice of two goals: (1) establish market leadership by making an early preemptive investment of $40 million in plant and equipment, or (2) attempt to win an upcoming major European space agency contract as a base load for the facility, a process that would take two years.

To establish market leadership, it would be necessary to sell products at cost to generate demand from commercial and industrial buyers. The investment would be justified then, on the basis that customers once signed on would stay as customers as prices later rose to provide an acceptable level of profitability. The necessary early years of low earnings, however, would result in a projected return below the corporate hurdle rate. So by default, the second goal became the operable one. Unfortunately, a French company – also seeing the value of the space agency business – fought tenaciously and won the contract on its home turf.

In the end, the U.S. company revised its market forecast and invested in a European plant anyway. But by then, two years had passed and the French were in the market with their own plant. The company had lost an opportunity to make strong, long-term profits; number crunching had gotten in the way of sound strategic judgment.

How much will the plan cost?

As a fourth and final step, the business manager must request the resources necessary to carry out the plan. Having established the plan, its rationale, and the goals, the manager now has to "cut the deal." In other words, for there to be real consensus and commitment, sufficient funds and personnel have to be allocated.

Failure to establish agreement on resources – monetary, human, and others – usually means the program will not be sustained. A major division presented a plan which called for making a $50 million acquisition in a closely related industry. There was no discussion, however, about creating the search and evaluation team needed to make the acquisition. Consequently, while the president accepted the program, no

> ## You don't have commitment until people and money are allocated.

human resources were allocated to accomplish the task. No acquisition was ever made.

The plan meeting is really the first step in the budget process. Does your CEO support programs during the plan meeting but cut back those same programs at budget time? The fact is, business managers frequently don't emphasize the cost impact of their initiatives, worried that the project might get killed before it gets off the ground. These are the same managers who complain of a lack of feedback and who cry foul when their budget requests are rejected.

I was once helping a divisional VP prepare the documentation for his annual meeting when it became obvious that he was uncomfortable with the spending level projected for a new initiative, about $3 million. If the planning process had been working effectively, he would either have gone back to the unit manager and negotiated a change or presented it to the president to get his opinion on the acceptable spending level. In this case, he did neither. He eliminated the initiative from his discussion. This "solution" actually undermined the plan. The business manager and the VP were left with neither the guidance nor the authority to carry it out.

The presenter must identify his or her current year's expenditures and compare them with the request for next year and for following years. Here, a financial staff is obviously not just a help in preparing the request; it's mandatory. There shouldn't be any surprises, and a budget increase should be linked to some specified payback – higher growth or an expanded market share.

Resource allocation discussions are about the short as well as the long term. They should address next year's budget for the project. Based on the CEO's response to anticipated spending levels, the business unit can better allocate its funding. Of course, it's not all engraved in stone. You'll have opportunities to reestablish the need for parts of the program that are to come in later years.

The payoff

The payoff from the preliminary meetings is an agenda that will get your boss to focus on the initiatives you have in mind. You should minimize the written requirements and encourage informality in your discussions.

All four agenda points should be addressed at the same meeting with the boss. I've seen managers talk about their plan and get agreement on goals, only to find out later that the money wasn't there or that the strategy was so vaguely worded that participants had conflicting interpretations of it. To know that you're on the same wavelength on all four points, they must all be resolved together.

This four-step procedure has been successfully used by business owners with $500,000 in sales and by divisional vice presidents representing $500 million. With such an agenda, the boss, the CEO – the decision maker – will be able to participate in the construction of your plan without spending an inordinate amount of time. Chances are, you'll get a decision. Moreover, the meeting's results will be simply stated so they can be communicated informally and rapidly to lower level managers, thus setting the backdrop for actions to be taken by the enterprise.

Reprint 88608

Effective Job
Interviewing

IDEAS FOR ACTION

ABCs of Job Interviewing

Preparation, via a scenario, is the key.

by James M. Jenks and Brian L.P. Zevnik

Your organization is looking over several candidates for a vacancy in its managerial ranks, and you have the final say in the decision. You are getting ready to interview the applicants.

Are you well prepared for this task? Poorly conducted interviews can come back to haunt you – you may hire someone who doesn't work out or reject someone with star potential. Or in these litigious days, you may risk being slapped with a lawsuit and hauled into court.

Unlike your human resources people, you interview applicants only occasionally. You don't catch that duty often enough to hone your skills. The candidates themselves are likely to be more adroit than you. Often they have received careful instructions from the recruiting firms that sent them your way. Recent experience on the job trail may have taught them all the right things to ask and say.

Then there are the personal attributes that you bring to the interview. The aggressive characteristics that helped put you in an executive position also put obstacles in your way to becoming an expert interviewer – learning how to ask, to watch, and to listen. The take-charge attitude of many top executives makes it hard for them to keep their ears open and mouths shut – two critical characteristics of the expert interviewer.

On the other hand, you know the job and the qualities you're looking for. Furthermore, your concern over having a good fit between individual and organization is your greatest advantage: with the proper preparation, it will give you an edge in the interview.

Prepping for the interviews

Before the interviews begin, write out a job profile based on the job description. The purpose is to translate duties and responsibilities into the personal characteristics the manager must have to do the job.

Take the job description for a national sales manager for a life insurance company. One duty is, "Reviews data to calculate sales potential and customer desires and to recommend prices and policies to meet sales goals." From that you distill these requirements for your profile: powers of analysis, managerial skills, commitment. Another duty, "Prepares periodic sales reports showing potential sales and actual results," calls for skill in writing and in oral communication.

Now you get down to specifics. For every duty or responsibility, you list the characteristics or qualities your candidate must possess to do the job. For instance, regarding powers of analysis: "Finds information in such publications as *Insurance and Tax News* and interprets it to show how sales agents can use tax law changes to sell life insurance policies." And concerning written communication: "Writes copy for advertising department to prepare new sales brochures for agents describing benefits of various types of life insurance for young singles, young newly marrieds, and mature empty nesters."

Naturally, you'll find that many requirements for different jobs are alike. Your human resources department can help in determining the most important characteristics and otherwise preparing you for the interviews.

Once you've listed the job requirements, put them in black and white: prepare a written interview guide. Using such a guide doesn't mean that you lack verbal facility, smoothness in meeting people, or deftness in leading a discussion; rather, it contributes substantially to a wise assessment of applicants with whom you must go one-on-one.

Here is a checklist of items as a basis for an interview guide:
☐ Consult the applicant's résumé and application for jobs, experience, accomplishments that are most relevant to your job requirements.
☐ Plan questions touching on the qualities you are looking for. In the interviews with applicants for insur-

James M. Jenks is chairman of the Alexander Hamilton Institute, which has purveyed employment relations information to organizations for 80 years. Brian L.P. Zevnik is its editor-in-chief. Jointly they wrote Managers Caught in the Crunch *(Franklin Watts, 1988).*

ance company national sales manager, if you know that a candidate indeed reads journals like *Insurance and Tax News*, you might probe: "Tell me how you've interpreted information from such publications for sales purposes."

☐ Prepare a step-by-step scenario of how to present the position.

☐ Do the same for your company, division, and department.

☐ Seek examples of behavior by focusing on what the applicant has done, not on what he or she might do. Of the life insurance sales manager applicant, you might ask: "Can you show me samples of brochures, sales letters, or articles you've developed?"

An interview guide will help you to be consistent and focused in your questioning, thus ensuring each applicant a fair shake, steering you clear of improper questions, and preventing you from putting applicants on the defensive. Moreover, an interview guide keeps you in control of the conversation.

Past performance

It has long been established that a person's past behavior is the surest guide to future performance. To determine an applicant's fit with the people in your company (including you) requires questions that uncover personality characteristics.

How can you make a judgment as to whether an applicant will do the job and fit in well? You are looking for a particular kind of behavior for every critical requirement you've listed for the job. The question to keep in mind is, What has this candidate done in the past to meet these requirements? So make a list of questions that are relevant to your concerns about them.

The following examples illustrate the kinds of questions that reveal willingness to do the job as well as style and personality:

Your concern: In this era of DINK (double income, no kids) couples, you may wonder about the prospective employee's motivation to work. Will this person put in the hours necessary to get the job done?

Faulty question: "Is your spouse employed?"

Comment: Such a question makes for amiable conversation, but it doesn't meet your concern. It has little to do with the candidate's motivation to work.

Improved questions: "Can you tell me about any project you had to

---

The executive's take-charge bent isn't conducive to effective interviewing.

---

tackle where you had to meet a hard deadline? What did you do to get the work out on time?"

When the individual you seek is one who can make an appreciable difference in the company, simply meeting the position's technical qualifications is not enough. You're not just filling a slot, you're hiring someone who is flexible, who will do what the job requires.

Your concern: How well this candidate will meet the demands of the position.

Faulty question: "Did you ever drop the ball on your last job and get bawled out by your boss?"

Comment: There are several problems with this question. For one thing, it can be answered with a single word—"yes" or "no." And a single-word answer (whichever it is) does nothing to get at your concern. Secondly, you're asking for a confession of failure, which is difficult for anyone to make. Finally, the question is unrelated to any requirement of the position and therefore gives you no behavioral matches.

Improved question: "Tell me about a task you took on in your previous job that would prepare you for handling the requirements we're discussing here."

Naturally, you want to consider how well the applicant will get along with colleagues as well as top executives—if the job opening is at a high level.

Your concern: How well the candidate will fit in your organization.

Faulty questions: "You need a lot of personal PR in this position. Do

you get along well with people? What clubs do you belong to?"

Comment: No matter how strong the candidates or how expert in their fields, if they don't work well in your particular environment, they'll fail. Some interviewers ask about hobbies and clubs to ascertain fit. But such questions stray into irrelevant areas. What does being a good tennis player have to do with getting along with peers or superiors?

Improved question: "Tell me about any incident in your last job that caused a conflict with another manager; what did you do to smooth things out?"

Assessment of how well candidates have mastered human relations skills is difficult. Interviewers often ask questions about activities that are at best only dimly connected to the position's requirements.

Your concern: On paper, your candidate for a professional position is well qualified. But the person selected will also direct a staff that includes several supervisors, so you need to find a candidate with good people-managing skills.

Faulty question: "What do you do on your own time, say, with clubs, associations, or groups of people?"

Comment: This question is designed to find out if the candidate is congenial and well rounded, but it promises to uncover nothing valuable about the candidate's behavior.

Improved questions: "We all run into instances where two people disagree on how to get a job done. Can you tell me how you handled a particular argument or disagreement about operations that came up among the people you managed in your last job? How about disputes between colleagues?"

Wrong and right tacks

Doing your homework thoroughly will help you maintain control of the dialogue and avoid pitfalls that interviewers often run into. Here are some "don'ts" in the art of interviewing.

Don't telegraph the response you're seeking. Suppose you are exploring the candidate's ability to work with departments that he or she would have no control over. "Do

Shooting the Rapids

The principle of fairness in employment, which has become the law of the land, does not ignore the seemingly straightforward job interview. Not only must you be sure that your hiring practices conform to legal specs but you must also take great care in your questions.

The dangerous questions aren't those that reflect overt discrimination. In any case, the law and its enforcers are more concerned with the effects of employers' actions than with their intentions. The dangerous questions are those meant to discover something interviewers *think* they need to know, something it would be *nice* to know, or even something intended to put the applicant at ease, like questions about family or nationality.

Executives ask irrelevant questions because they reason that the information may be useful should the job seeker become an employee. Questions that can be asked after hire, concerning age and marital status, for example, may be illegal during pre-employment interviews. (Technically, a question

by itself usually isn't illegal. It's when the answers are improperly used that the *gendarmes* swarm in.)

Suppose an executive asks a female applicant this seemingly innocuous question: "What kind of work does your husband do?" He wants to put her at ease and at the same time get an inkling about how long the candidate might want to stay on the job. But the question is patently discriminatory because it is seldom asked of males. Moreover, it is irrelevant to the job requirements or the person's qualifications.

Our society seems intent on using the courts as the first resort, not the last, to redress suffering. Corporations and executives are being dragged into court with dismaying frequency, and juries are awarding enormous sums – even into the millions – against both "deep pockets" corporations and individual executives.

The key to preventing discrimination claims lies in one simple policy. If a question is not directly related to the hiring decision and relevant to the job, don't ask it.

to be at work by 8 A.M. At unscheduled times each month, you'll have to come to executive committee meetings beginning at 5 P.M. and lasting several hours. How do you feel about that kind of unpredictable schedule?"

Don't get into a joust. Some people revel in one-upmanship or competitive tilting. You wonder whether this candidate is willing to work what are usually leisure hours to complete projects within deadline, so you ask, "Would you work weekends and holidays when necessary?" Your applicant fires back, "Absolutely. I can keep up with anybody else's schedule."

Implicit in this thrust is the claim that he or she can do anything you can do. Feel your hackles rising? Avoid that kind of behavior with straightforward business questions. Keep your feelings in check and your combativeness on a short leash. A better tack would be, "How do you plan your week's activities? Tell me what you do in your current job when you can't meet your planned schedule."

Finally, don't get uptight if the applicant gets uptight. You control the situation, it's your show. Part of your job is to make the interview an informative meeting, not a trip to the dentist's chair. Remember too that part of your task is to sell your organization to a top-notch candidate. You do that with convincing descriptions of the position, the opportunities, and the organization itself; also by how you come across – natural, prepared, professional. Furthermore, if you get uptight, you're liable to do too much talking and not enough listening.

Hiring is like a contest, especially when you're engaging skillful players who are the kind you always want on your managerial team. Choosing the right applicants for important management slots is a key to achieving exceptional results for you and your company. Behavioral-match, performance-oriented questions, buttressed by careful preparation, give you the best chance of finding talented candidates who will do more than just fill those slots well.

you think you'll be able to get cooperation from managers in other areas of the company?" you ask. The applicant smoothly replies, "No problem. I get along with everybody."

Your question not only allows a sharp interviewee to give you the response you want to hear but also gives you zero help in finding out what you really want to know. We suggest something like: "Tell me about a time when you had to gain the cooperation of a group you had no authority over. What did you do?"

Don't get defensive if an interviewee directs a tough question right back at you. You may be concerned,

for example, about the person's steady availability. So you ask, "Do you have any small children at home?" She replies easily, "I think you'll agree that my experience and education clearly show I'm qualified. I'm not at all sure why you asked that question. Can you explain?" The applicant has neatly lobbed the ball back into your court and put you on the defensive. (And since the question is rarely asked of males, it borders on illegality anyway. See the insert "Shooting the Rapids.")

A better approach would be: "I don't know if you're aware of this, but we need managers at your level

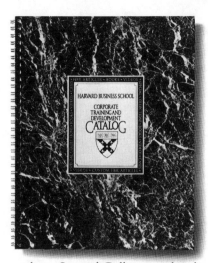